30
Meditations
on
HEALING

30 Meditations on HEALING

Marilyn Hickey
& Sarah Bowling

WHITAKER
HOUSE

Unless otherwise indicated, all Scripture quotations are taken from the *New King James Version*, © 1979, 1980, 1982, 1984 by Thomas Nelson, Inc. Used by permission. All rights reserved. Scripture quotations marked (KJV) are taken from the King James Version of the Holy Bible. Scripture quotations marked (NIV) are taken from the *Holy Bible, New International Version*˚, NIV˚, © 1973, 1978, 1984 by the International Bible Society. Used by permission of Zondervan. All rights reserved. Scripture quotations marked (MESSAGE) are taken from *The Message: The Bible in Contemporary Language* by Eugene H. Peterson, © 1993, 1994, 1995, 1996, 2000, 2001, 2002. Used by permission of NavPress Publishing Group. All rights reserved.

Boldface type in Scripture quotations indicates the emphasis of the author.

Some definitions of Hebrew and Greek words are taken from the electronic versions of *Strong's Exhaustive Concordance of the Bible*, STRONG, (© 1980, 1986, and assigned to World Bible Publishers, Inc. Used by permission. All rights reserved.) or the *New American Standard Exhaustive Concordance of the Bible*, NASC, (© 1981 by The Lockman Foundation. Used by permission. All rights reserved.).

30 MEDITATIONS ON HEALING

Marilyn Hickey Ministries
P.O. Box 6598
Englewood, CO 80155
www.marilynandsarah.org

ISBN: 978-1-60374-995-4
eBook ISBN: 978-1-60374-996-1
Printed in the United States of America
© 2014 by Marilyn Hickey Ministries

Whitaker House
1030 Hunt Valley Circle
New Kensington, PA 15068
www.whitakerhouse.com

Library of Congress Cataloging-in-Publication Data (Pending)

1 2 3 4 5 6 7 8 9 10 11 WH 20 19 18 17 16 15 14

FOREWORD

In the twenty-first century, meditation has become a lost spiritual discipline.

During the time of Christ, some rabbinic schools required students to memorize the entire Torah, or at least the Pentateuch. In the Middle Ages, individuals memorized the entire book of Psalms. Jesus overcame temptation through memorized Scripture. The apostles quoted Scripture in their sermons and in their writings.

Today, many followers of Christ have electronic versions of the Bible loaded onto their phones, their iPads, and their computers, as well as dust-covered physical Bibles, stacked on bookshelves; but few followers of Christ systematically meditate upon the Word of God.

Marilyn Hickey has personally inspired me to meditate on the Word of God. I know her teachings will inspire you, too.

—*Dr. Darryl Wootton*
Lead Pastor, First Assembly of God
Bartlesville, Oklahoma

CONTENTS

INTRODUCTION

MEDITATING:
THE #1 KEY TO SUCCESS

Hide-and-seek was a fun game. I can hear the refrain: "Ready or not, here I come!" One child was "it," and he would cover his eyes on home base as all the other children ran and hid. The object was for those who were hiding to get "home" before they were found.

It was great entertainment, and amusing, but there's a "hiding" that is essential to our walk as Christians that I want to present here.

I'm referring to hiding the Word in our hearts, and the "who, what, when, where, and how" of doing this. The Bible says, "*Your word I have hidden in my heart, that I might not sin against You!*" (Psalm 119:11). When we hide the Word in our hearts, it not only keeps us from sin, as the psalmist said, but it also will bring success.

Most promises in the Bible relate to specific actions:

"Honor your father and mother," which is the first command-
ment with promise: "that it may be well with you and you may
live long on the earth."   (Ephesians 6:2–3)

The command (action) involves honoring your parents, and it is accompanied by a specific promise: that you may be well and *"live long on the earth."*

God gave a command to Joshua. It was given because of God's promise to lead Israel into the Promised Land. After forty years in the wilderness, Joshua was chosen to fulfill the hundreds-of-years-old pledge. In Joshua 1:8, he received a command to meditate. The instruction was for *all people*, as you'll see from reading further Scriptures on meditation, and it carries a promise that goes with everything in your life. This Scripture enlightens us about hiding the Word. It says,

> *This Book of the Law shall not depart from your mouth, but you shall meditate in it day and night, that you may observe to do according to all that is written in it. For then you will make your way prosperous, and then you will have good success.*
>
> (Joshua 1:8)

God said, in effect, "If you meditate on My Word, day and night, and if you speak that Word and obey it, everything in your life will be prosperous and successful!"

I've discovered that God has a lot to say about meditating, and I've become excited about what meditating on His Word accomplishes. It is important that you understand what meditation is and what it will do for you. Meditating on God's Word changes lives—in fact, it *is* life.

I've heard many testimonies regarding the effects of medication. If you know me, I'm sure most of you know Sarah Bowling. She's a wife, a mother, a teacher of the Word, a pastor, and my television cohost on *Today with Marilyn and Sarah*. And, if you did not know, she is my daughter. She ministers alongside Reece Bowling, her husband, who is senior pastor of Orchard Road Christian Center, in Greenwood, Colorado. The crux of her heart's cry is a ministry she founded, called Saving Moses, which concentrates on saving young children, from newborns to the age of five.

Sarah's life has been strongly affected by meditation. This is what she says:

> The most powerful experience I've had meditating on the Bible was when I was in my early twenties. I was spending the summer doing missions work in Hong Kong. At the time, I was a schoolteacher and had made some bad decisions in my personal life during the preceding school year. During my time there, I was not only involved in missions work but I also was trying to get past the dilemma created by those choices. Thankfully, I had supportive people around me and made great friendships.
>
> Over the course of that summer, what helped my thinking the most was my experience with memorizing and meditating on Colossians 3. I found that the longer I memorized and meditated on those verses, the more healthy my mind and thoughts became. As I continued to progress through the chapter, it felt as though the verses I memorized were figuratively washing out all the garbage those bad decisions had deposited in my mind. Furthermore, it felt like those verses were not only cleaning my mind, but they also were replacing destructive mindsets with more truth-oriented thoughts and convictions.
>
> I've never forgotten that experience and the transforming power of meditating on the Bible. Subsequently, I've used the principles of meditating over the course of my life with equally powerful results and transformations.

I'm sure most of you are familiar with Rick Warren's book *The Purpose Driven Life*. Rick is the founder and senior pastor of

Saddleback Church, in Forest Lake, California. This is what he said in his book about meditation:

Meditation is "thinking about God"—His essence, His desires, His plans, His mercy, etc.—throughout each day. And the only way a Christian can do this is by knowing God—and the only way a Christian can know God is through His Word. Meditation (similar to the process of "worrying"), which is only "focused thinking," is accomplished when one mulls over (contemplates, ponders) God's Word continually during the day.

Meditation allows God to share His secrets (revelations) with His children—to speak to His children in a close and personal way. To properly meditate requires a life of studying God's thoughts recorded in the Bible. It also means that a Christian should continuously review biblical truths when they are presented in sermons, radio broadcasts, Bible studies, etc."[1]

Meditation isn't always easy, and it's no small wonder the enemy has desperately tried to mask the topic of meditation on God's Word. He's brought in many counterfeits, such as transcendental meditation, and all kinds of distraction. Whenever you see the devil putting up a smokescreen, you can be sure he's counterfeiting something real. The devil never created anything. All he can do is falsify and imitate what already exists.

---

1. Rick Warren, *The Purpose Driven Life* (Grand Rapids, MI: Zondervan, 2002), 85.

1

THE "WHO" OF MEDITATION

I mentioned earlier God's promise for success in Joshua 1:8.

What is success? Let's look at the Hebrew word for *"prosperous"*: *tsalach*.

It means:

1. to rush

2. to advance, prosper, make progress, succeed, be profitable

3. to make prosperous, bring to successful issue, cause to prosper

4. to show or experience prosperity, prosper

You see how success and prosperity go hand in hand? This Hebrew word has the correct signification. When I read "to advance," I think of wading across a river or pushing forward toward a goal. Proverbs 13:19 says, *"A desire accomplished is sweet to the soul."*

Another meaning of this word is "to fall upon." Picture God's riches falling upon you. Also hidden in this good word is the meaning "to finish well." God's Word has happy endings.

Lastly, it can be translated as "promote." The Hebrew connotation means it brings promotion.

If you so desired, you could place "meditate" before each meaning and make an equation straight across the line. Do you want to prosper as a wife, a husband, a mother, an employer, an employee, a friend, a sweetheart, a neighbor, a minister, or as a Christian? Meditation on God's Word is the unusual key that unlocks all of His success. It is the solution, and we need to know what it is and how to do it.

Many will say that this passage was written only for Joshua. They may say, "Well, God gave Joshua success because he had to take the Promised Land." But I want to tell you that God did more than tell us to take the Promised Land—He told us to take the world for Jesus.

Meditation can dramatically change your life. In this passage, God is talking about a "blessed man." He says:

> *Blessed is the man who walks not in the counsel of the ungodly, nor stands in the path of sinners, nor sits in the seat of the scornful; but his delight is in the law of the LORD, and in His law he meditates day and night. He shall be like a tree planted by the rivers of water, that brings forth its fruit in its season, whose leaf also shall not wither; and whatever he does shall prosper.* (Psalm 1:1–3)

If you meditate on the Word day and night, you'll implement the key element of being blessed, prosperous, and successful in every area of your life.

"Oh," you say, "there's that ugly word *meditate*." I think some Christians have this word confused with *medicate*. I think they associate it with a task that is time-consuming and difficult. However, meditation does not need to be drudgery. Rather, I have discovered that it adds a *refreshing* quality to my study of God's

Word. It is my desire for you to see transformation take place when you begin applying the principles of meditation to your own life. As Rick Warren suggested, if you know how to worry, you already know how to meditate!

In the passage above, we run into the same idea found in Joshua 1:8. *"Blessed is the man...."* The man who meditated on the Word will be prosperous and successful in all that he does. Shall we embrace the truth of meditating? Or shall we simply stand aside and, with words and acts, watch other Christians meditate? We are too busy, too old, or too "out of it" to be bothered.

However, you see, Psalm 1 whets every believer's appetite for meditation. It states, *"Blessed is the man who...meditates"* (Psalm 1:1–2). The word *blessedness* is not found in the Hebrew text, because there is no such thing as a singular blessing, only plural blessings. Psalm 1 says that meditating will give you vitality *"like a tree"* (Psalm 1:3). It will give you security, for you will be *"planted"* (verse 3). Your capacity will be unlimited because His sources are *"the rivers* [plural] *of water"* (verse 3). You will be fertile, because meditating *"brings forth its fruit"* (verse 3). You will have seasons and perpetuate, because your *"leaf...shall not wither"* (verse 3). What prosperity! Everything you do *"shall prosper"* (verse 3).

Can you look into the mirror of these words and see yourself?

Because of the blessings, successes, and revelations I've received, I've condensed hours of study, practical experience, and character studies on meditation, which I believe will compel you to meditate on His Word—letting it dominate and change your life for the better. I pray the Lord will throw open the shutters of your spiritual understanding so that you may receive all the blessings He has for you in the fullness of His Word.

Let this truth be gladly received in your mind and your will. Embrace this truth. There's only one way to go—forward!

2

THE "WHAT" OF MEDITATION

*"This Book of the Law shall not depart from your mouth, but
you shall meditate in it day and night, that you may observe to
do according to all that is written in it. For then you will make
your way prosperous, and then you will have good success."*
—Joshua 1:8

M*editate*—a word abused, misused, and charged by Christians
as an unscriptural principle. Yet God spoke to Joshua, saying that
if he would not allow His Word to depart out of his mouth, but
instead meditate on it day and night, observing to do it, He would
make everything Joshua put his hands to prosper and be successful. It's a simple thing for us to rationalize and simply pass off the
strong admonition given to Joshua. It's easy to insist that the command was for Joshua only. After all, he had a big Promised Land
to conquer. However, lest we speak too lightly of such words, Jesus
told us to conquer a gigantic world with His Word. If meditation on the Word conquered Canaan, a land of giants, as well as
walled cities, and brought forth milk and honey, could it conquer

our giants, bring down the walls of our opposition, and pour forth milk and honey into our daily lives? Could we, too, conquer a world of Canaanites, as Joshua did?

What is meditation? It is to chew, to mutter, to memorize, visualize, and personalize the Word of God. Meditation presents a zealous promise that is tremendous in scope.

Genesis 24:63 is the first reference to meditation recorded in the Bible: *"And Isaac went out to meditate in the field in the evening; and he lifted his eyes and looked, and there, the camels were coming."*

It was the first time Isaac laid eyes on his beloved Rebekah, and it was love at first sight. And it happened as he was meditating.

What can we glean from this initial reference? It says, Isaac *"lifted his eyes."* I've found lifting your eyes will help you to see Jesus in your circumstances. When Abraham *"lifted his eyes,"* he received a divine visitation. He also *"lifted his eyes"* (Genesis 22:13) when Isaac was delivered from being sacrificed on Mount Moriah.

God's promises were incubated with Abram (who later became Abraham). He spoke to Abram the first time and told him to do three things:

1. Leave the city of Ur.

2. Don't take relatives.

3. Go to the Promised Land.

God told Abram he would receive specific blessings for obeying. When he fully obeyed these three commands, he received the blessings (promises) the Lord set forth. Even though he didn't see them all come about in his lifetime, he received them nonetheless.

As we know, Abraham wanted Isaac to have a righteous wife. He didn't want him to marry any Canaanite women. We'll see why later. So, he called for his servant, who took a vow to find the right woman. He found Rebekah and brought her to meet Isaac.

As we read, the Bible tells us that Isaac was meditating in the field. Now this happened at night, mind you, when one wouldn't anticipate anyone coming to his home. Isaac lifted his eyes. What caused him to do this? It was dark, and he probably couldn't see very well. Don't you think his meditation had something to do with it?

The Hebrew word used here for *meditation* is used only once in the Bible: *suwach*. It means "to muse," which is to ponder, consider, or mull over. So here we have Isaac, at the end of the day, in the field by himself. What a lonely portrait. However, he was most likely ruminating on the promises God gave to his father, Abraham. God's pledge to him was,

> *I will make you a great nation; I will bless you and make your name great; and you shall be a blessing. I will bless those who bless you, and I will curse him who curses you; and in you all the families of the earth shall be blessed.*   (Genesis 12:2–3)

These promises included assurances of another land, another nation, and a spiritual blessing for generations to come. They were great and mighty promises, and they required that Isaac marry the right woman. No doubt, it weighed heavy on his shoulders as he deliberated. That evening, his answer came; God solved his dilemma.

How is that going to help you? Lift up your eyes. The Lord knows the perfect one for you. You don't. Maybe you're already married, and you don't need a mate. Lift up your eyes and thank God for the mate you have. But know that as you meditate on His promises, He will bring them to pass. I love how God works.

To meditate gives forth the flavorful meaning of being separated, as the dross is separated from the silver. So, must a man separate himself from the crowd in order to help the crowd? Isn't that goofy? Proverbs 25:4 says, *"Take away the dross from the silver, and there shall come forth a vessel for the finer"* (KJV).

Psalm 119:15 says, *"I will meditate on Your precepts, and contemplate Your ways."* It gives the idea of bowing down and musing. There is the idea of a pilgrimage in this word. Imagine, taking a trip into God's Word. Fantastic!

Lastly is the concept of Psalm 39:3, *"My heart was hot within me; while I was musing, the fire burned. Then I spoke with my tongue."* It infers the focusing of the rays of God's love and power on a man's heart, which starts a fire, before the tongue begins to speak. This sums up the process of taking the Word, speaking it, walking with it, and allowing it to guide you.

Bill Gothard has stated that meditating is: (1) to memorize, (2) to personalize, and (3) to spiritualize. How precise and true.

As you see, to meditate is to walk and talk. Plan on becoming a spiritual "walkie-talkie."

Scriptures on meditation say that if you meditate on the Word, keeping it in your mind, letting it go from there to your mouth, and acting on it, you will be successful spiritually, physically, mentally, and emotionally. As a parent, a spouse, a child, a cook, or a student—no matter what you do—you will be prosperous if you obey the command in Joshua 1:8. This is a Scripture key in the Bible that carries tremendous impact.

Three Components of Joshua 1:8

As we continue to look at what meditation is, we see three parts to Joshua 1:8.

Part one involves your mouth: *"This Book of the Law shall not depart from your mouth."*

The Message version reads, *"And don't for a minute let this Book of The Revelation be out of mind"* (Joshua 1:8 MESSAGE).

You have to spend time thinking the Word first, which, of course, comes by reading. Please realize that as you memorize a Scripture, it is for you. Visualize it in your mind's eye. Part two involves the meditation itself: *"You shall meditate in it day and night."* I mentioned *to mutter* earlier. The Hebrew word *meditate* translates as "to moan, growl, utter, muse, mutter, meditate, devise, plot, and speak." Remember that meditation involves "talking" God's Word, or muttering. By doing this, you will fulfill the first part of this command, and then you will not let it depart from your mouth. You may say, "Wait a minute. You're telling me to speak, but also that it won't depart from my mouth." Yes, when you mutter the word and speak it to yourself, it will become ingrained in your brain, rooted in your mind. It won't depart from you, I promise.

Part three brings in the action: *"...that you may observe to do according to all that is written in it."* Meditation not only involves thinking and talking, but it also involves walking. We are to be doers of God's Word, not hearers only. (See James 1:22.)

These three elements of meditation bring forth the promise, *"...then you will make your way prosperous, and then you will have good success."*

Many people say, "If only there was something that I could do about this terrible situation." What can you do? Meditate on the Word.

God did not say, "If you'll do this, I'll make your way prosperous." He said, in effect, "If you'll meditate, *you* will make your way prosperous." That is a big difference. You alone are the deciding factor. God will never force you to meditate on His Word; neither will He force prosperity on you. Meditation on God's Word is a consuming effort, not merely a pastime.

The word *meditate* in the above Scripture means to speak with oneself in a low voice, or to think aloud on the Word of God. This keeps the mind saturated with God's truth so that it can give a proper answer.

Joshua Affected Three Ways

There's something interesting about the first chapter of the book of Joshua. There are three separate places in the chapter where God told Joshua to be strong and courageous.

The first instance is in Joshua 1:6:

Be strong and of good courage, for to this people you shall divide as an inheritance the land which I swore to their fathers to give them.

This command appears in two other places:

Only be strong and very courageous, that you may observe to do according to all the law which Moses My servant commanded you; do not turn from it to the right hand or to the left, that you may prosper wherever you go.   (verse 7)

Have I not commanded you? Be strong and of good courage; do not be afraid, nor be dismayed, for the LORD your God is with you wherever you go.   (verse 9)

That bothered me at first. I wondered, *Why does God tell Joshua to be strong and courageous three times in the same chapter that He tells Joshua to meditate on the Word?* Then I looked carefully at those verses, and I realized that God wanted Joshua to be strong and courageous in three different ways:

1.   In his body

2. In his spirit

3. In his soul (his mind, emotions, and will)

First, let's see how God wanted to strengthen Joshua physically. When the Lord told him to capture the Promised Land for his people, Joshua was more than eighty years old. He was going to need supernatural strength to take that land. And he received strength in his body; and you will, too.

Then, in Joshua 1:7, the Lord spoke about Joshua's spirit. He said, *"Do not turn from it to the right hand or to the left."* Just stay with it, and receive it into your spirit. Joshua received strength and courage in his spirit. This Scripture pertains to all of us.

Finally, God spoke to Joshua about having strength and courage in his soul when He said, *"Do not be afraid, nor be dismayed"* (Joshua 1:9). God wanted to bind Joshua with the wonderful strength provided through His Word in every area of his life. Joshua received strength through meditation, and so can you.

A Foundation

Since God told Joshua that meditation on the Word would make him prosperous and successful, I decided to study Joshua's life, and I saw that the "proof of the pudding is in the eating." After examining his life, I discovered that meditation had a definite impact on all that Joshua did. Before we look at how this occurred, I want you to understand what is involved.

Changes in Your Life

Are there areas in your life that need changed or a refreshed? The Bible says if you meditate on the Word of God day and night, you'll be prosperous and successful in every area of your life. The

Word profited my very first meditation partner in the area of her personality, because she considered the Word, instead of her problems. It was tremendous to see the transformation that occurred in her life. I want to challenge you to meditate on the Word of God and see how it will change your life, too. Meditation isn't just for Joshua, and it isn't just for pastors—it's for you, too!

Three Basic Steps

The three basic steps of meditation are:

1. Memorize

2. Personalize

3. Visualize

Memorize

If you're like most people, you may get uptight as soon as you hear the word *memorize*. Some people say, "I'm beyond forty years old; I can't memorize anymore." Don't say that. The Bible says you have the mind of Christ. (See 1 Corinthians 2:16.) In John 14:26, Jesus promised, *"But the Helper, the Holy Spirit, whom the Father will send in My name, He will teach you all things, and bring to your remembrance all things that I said to you."* This is very important: How can the Holy Spirit bring something to your remembrance if there is nothing to remember? You are to memorize God's Word so that He can make you remember.

Personalize

As you meditate, don't just say, "This is God's Word to all Christians." You should say, "This is God's Word for *me*!" Some people read the Bible as though it's for everybody but them. God isn't a respecter of persons. (See Acts 10:34 KJV.) That means that He is not more interested in other people. His promises are for you.

Visualize

You must see God's Word as finished. See His Word happening in your life, in spite of what your circumstances may look like. I call visualization "faith sight." Visualization is found in the life of Abraham:

> By faith Abraham, when he was tested, offered up Isaac, and he who had received the promises offered up his only begotten son, of whom it was said, "In Isaac your seed shall be called," concluding that God was able to raise him up, even from the dead, from which he also received him in a figurative sense.
> (Hebrews 11:17–19)

When Abraham was on his way to offer Isaac to the Lord as a sacrifice of consecration, he told his servants, "*Stay here with the donkey; the lad and I will go yonder and worship, and we will come back to you*" (Genesis 22:5). What was Abraham saying? He was visualizing God's promise to bless his seed—Isaac, his son. He was seeing God's Word as complete truth, and saying, in effect, "Even if I do sacrifice Isaac and God has to resurrect him from the ashes, He has made me a promise, and He will keep it." Abraham was seeing God's Word as complete, through visualization, which caused him to receive Isaac "in a figure."

When you meditate on the Word, begin saying what God says; accept His Word as a reality in your life; visualize it happening.

Have you ever daydreamed? Everybody has. You can have a spiritual dream by visualizing God's Word as if it were already accomplished in your life. This is the final step involved in the threefold process of meditation: first, you memorize; second, you personalize; and third, you visualize the results.

Joshua's Life of Meditation

Joshua's life was a testimony of the power of meditation and the blessings that it brings. Even in his mistakes, he was still prosperous and successful.

One of his mistakes was allowing himself to be deceived by some Gibeonite people. Gibeonites came from the Hivite tribe. *Hivite* means "snake" or "serpent." The Gibeonites were living in the land where the children of Israel were. It's easy to see why Hivite means "snake," because these people were crafty.

> *But when the inhabitants of Gibeon heard what Joshua had done to Jericho and Ai, they worked craftily, and went and pretended to be ambassadors. And they took old sacks on their donkeys, old wineskins torn and mended, old and patched sandals on their feet, and old garments on themselves; and all the bread of their provision was dry and moldy. And they went to Joshua, to the camp at Gilgal, and said to him and to the men of Israel, "We have come from a far country; now therefore, make a covenant with us."* (Joshua 9:3–6)

God distinctly warned Joshua not to make a covenant with the Gibeonites; but when they came to him, he didn't realize who they were, and he entered into a covenant with them.

> *They said to Joshua, "We are your servants." And Joshua said to them, "Who are you, and where do you come from?" So they said to him: "From a very far country your servants have come, because of the name of the LORD your God; for we have heard of His fame, and all that He did in Egypt, and all that He did to the two kings of the Amorites who were beyond the Jordan; to Sihon king of Heshbon, and Og king of Bashan, who was at Ashtaroth."* (Joshua 9:8–10)

The Gibeonites were intimidated by the Israelites, having heard about their victories in past battles. They wanted to be assured of favor and protection, which they would be guaranteed through a covenant.

Joshua made a covenant with them, and three days later, he received news that made him angry:

And it happened at the end of three days, after they had made a covenant with them, that they heard that they were their neighbors who dwelt near them.   (Joshua 9:16)

Now what would Joshua do? This did not look like a prosperous situation. The people said, *"We have sworn to them by the LORD God of Israel; now therefore, we may not touch them"* (Joshua 9:19). The Lord knew Joshua was a man of the Word. He had caused the Gibeonites to be their servants, and their descendants were a group of people called the Nethinims, meaning "devoted men of God."

After the children of Israel made a league with the Gibeonites, a king of Jerusalem heard about the victories that the Lord had given the Israelites. He also heard that the Israelites had covenanted with the Gibeonites, and, because Gibeon was a great city, he felt threatened. He sent armies to make war against Gibeon, but the men of camp called on Joshua:

Do not forsake your servants; come up to us quickly, save us and help us, for all the kings of the Amorites who dwell in the mountains have gathered together against us.   (Joshua 10:6)

What happened? God protected the Israelites and their servants. First, He sent hail that only hit the attacking army. Then, He sent confusion and ambush, which caused them to fight against each other. And something else happened that made this day unique to its kind:

Then Joshua spoke to the Lord...*and he said in the sight of*
Israel: "Sun, stand still over Gibeon; and moon, in the Valley
of Aijalon." So the sun stood still, and the moon stopped, till
the people had revenge upon their enemies.

(Joshua 10:12–13)

When Joshua spoke, even the sun and the moon stood still.
Here is a man who kept God's powerful Word in his mouth all the
time. Joshua meditated on the Word and moved in its authority.

Do you need the power and strength of God in your life? Do
you want to be prosperous? The key is meditation.

Then I wondered, *What about Joshua's financial statement?*
He was successful physically, because he led the Israelites to take the
Promised Land, and it only took them six-and-a-half years to take it.
Was Joshua financially successful?

Many people imagine the children of Israel to be dressed
in rags, owning next to nothing, as they wandered through the
land. That is not so. When the Israelites cast lots to determine
where people would settle, according to their tribes, Joshua did
not choose some little old tent. No. He asked for the city Timnath
Serah (see Joshua 19:50), which means "the city of the sun." Joshua
owned a whole mountain with a city on top of it. Some would say,
"I'm going to be humble; just give me a little nest in the west."
Joshua received a double portion of wealth. Why? Because his priority was the Word of God.

If you are in the ministry, there are those who may wonder
about your family. Once, when I was teaching in a church, a big,
tall, Church-of-God minister stood up, turned to me and said, "I'd
like to ask you, what does your husband think about you traveling all over the countryside?" I thought, *Oh, God, give me a good*
answer. Then I asked him, "Which husband?" Everybody laughed,
and that night, he came forward after the service and received

the baptism of the Holy Spirit. People always wonder about your family when you're in the ministry, and I wondered the same thing about Joshua's family. The Lord showed me the answer, too. It's in Joshua 24:15–16:

> [Joshua said,] *"But as for me and my house, we will serve the* Lord." *So the people answered and said: "Far be it from us that we should forsake the* Lord *to serve other gods."*

Joshua and his family served the Lord. And what happened? They inspired all of the people of Israel to serve the Lord, too. A family that diligently seeks after God will bring Him glory, and meditating on God's Word will bring you total success in your family life.

Sometimes in my own life, when situations have appeared impossible, I've reminded the Lord, "You said that if I meditated on Your Word day and night, my way would be prosperous and successful. That includes my children."

Meanings of *Meditate*

The word *meditate* is translated from three Hebrew words and two Greek words. One of the Hebrew words, *hagah*, found in both Joshua 1:8 and Psalm 1:2, means "to speak to one's self in a low voice," "to think out loud the Word of God," and "to keep the mind saturated with truth for a proper answer." *Meditate* can also mean "to separate the dross from the silver," as used in Proverbs 25:4: *"Take away the dross from the silver, and there shall come forth a vessel for the finer."*

Why separate the dross from the silver? To purify it. Meditation brings forth a cleansing; it is the washing of the water of the Word. How does a silversmith know that the silver is pure when he separates it from the dross? Because he can see his image reflected in it. Meditating on the Word of God will cleanse and purify you, so that His image will be reflected in all that you do. Your personality will be more like His than ever before, and you will be prosperous and successful in all that you do. You'll be *"a vessel for the finer."*

There's a beautiful picture formed by the Hebrew word *hagah.* The first letter, as it's written in Hebrew, is He, which stands for grace. The second is Gimel, which means "camel," and the third is He again. The depiction we see is grace, a camel to travel, and another level of grace. You may say that God gives us the means (the camel) to travel from grace to grace. Remember Genesis 24:63, when Isaac was meditating in the field in the evening? He lifted his eyes and, behold, camels were coming.

Just as Isaac bowed in reverence to the Lord, you, too, can literally bow in holy reverence to Him as you meditate; this is a precious practice. If you are meditating in a place where bowing is impossible, I believe you can "bow in your spirit" unto Him. It is a state of giving Him total control, when your mind, spirit, and body are subject to the Lord.

In this verse of Scripture, Isaac bowed and mused over God's Word. As I said earlier, when he lifted his eyes, camels approached, bringing him his bride. How wonderful it must have been: The first time Rebekah ever saw her husband, he was meditating on the Word of God.

Also recall Psalm 39:3, which offers another concept of meditation: *"My heart was hot within me; while I was musing, the fire burned. Then I spoke with my tongue."* The word *muse* means to meditate, and it focuses on God's love and power, starting a fire in a man's heart, causing him to speak. Jeremiah once refused to speak the Word of God, but then he said, *"But His word was in my heart like a burning fire shut up in my bones; I was weary of holding it back, and I could not"* (Jeremiah 20:9).

In Luke 24:32, the disciples saw Jesus after His ascension, and they said, *"Did not our heart burn within us while He talked with us on the road, and while He opened the Scriptures to us?"*

The Word of God will start a spiritual fire within you, and then it will cause you to utter words and articulate sounds with your voice. Meditate on the Word of God, and let it come out as fire, burning the chaff out of your life.

Meditating is supremely the most important thing that you, as a Christian, can do.

3

THE "WHEN" OF MEDITATION

Meditation carries the highest level of importance. The following Scripture provides a key for *when* we should meditate:

> *My son, keep your father's command, and do not forsake the law of your mother. Bind them continually upon your heart; tie them around your neck. When you roam, they will lead you; when you sleep, they will keep you; and when you awake, they will speak with you.* (Proverbs 6:20–22)

I memorize Scripture first thing in the morning, even before I brush my teeth. It's the best time, because my mind is clear and fresh. I recall my Scriptures early in the afternoon, because God's Word guides me. Then, the last thing I do before I go to sleep is say my Scriptures for the day aloud once again. You'll read more about this in chapter 5—the "How" section.

That final time I speak the Scripture, it saturates my very being. Solomon spoke these words to his people: *"Let your heart therefore be loyal to the* LORD *our God, to walk in His statutes and keep His commandments, as at this day"* (1 Kings 8:61). You say this takes discipline. You are so right. Isn't discipline worth it when it makes you prosperous and successful in all you do?

One night, a woman broke into our house when I was there alone. Actually, our toy poodle was with me, but that wasn't going to be of much help. However, God delivered me.

Several passages in the Bible talk about deliverance from evil by the blood of Jesus. (See Hebrews 2:14; Colossians 1:13; 2:15; 1 John 3:8; Revelation 12:11.) I had memorized this verse: *"He has delivered us from the power of darkness and conveyed us into the kingdom of the Son of His love"* (Colossians 1:13). I spoke this Word and found that it kept me; and I was delivered, praise be to God.

There are days when Scripture memorization goes easily and every taste of His Word in my mouth is delicious. But then there are days when it's hard; it feels drab and discouraging. There are times of tremendous pressure on my time and energy, and there are times when my mind is fuzzy with exhaustion. There are also times when the enemy whispers, *What is this proving?* However, beyond all of this is, "The entrance of His Word gives light" (see Psalm 119:130)—a light I've never known before.

Job stored the Word, and it became gold in his heart:

> *Receive, please, instruction from His mouth, and lay up His words in your heart. If you return to the Almighty, you will be built up; you will remove iniquity far from your tents. Then you will lay your gold in the dust, and the gold of Ophir among the stones of the brooks.*   (Job 22:22–24)

David said, *"My soul shall be satisfied as with marrow and fatness, and my mouth shall praise You with joyful lips. When I remember You on my bed, I meditate on You in the night watches"* (Psalm 63:5–6). He found that meditating at night brought richness to his soul. His meditation brought him through tremendous trials.

I once spoke with a lovely pastor's wife in Rapid City, South Dakota, and she told me, "I have started an 'M&M Club' in our church; it means *Memorize* and *Meditate*." She said, "There are sixteen of us that meet once a week, and we have memory partners. We get together to encourage each other with revelations that we've received during the week." She shared a lot of things about meditation with me that God had revealed to me, too. She spoke of how the Word of God had literally transformed them.

Meditating takes the Word and makes it glow within you; it puts fire in your mouth. It will put lightness in your steps and brightness in your eyes. The saturating of your spirit in the Word will conquer old problems and make new victories a reality. I've yet to meet one person who was sorry they memorized and meditated on the Word of God. You won't be sorry either.

Key Moments

One time, I took a private plane to a seminar in Billings, Montana. We departed early in the morning and decided to return home late that night. That evening, the plane would not start. The pilot said, "Oh, it's the battery." Someone was sent to recharge it, but when the plane finally rolled down the runway, one of the women onboard said, "The wheel on my side is on fire."

I looked out the window on my side and confirmed that the wheel was indeed on fire, and I told the pilot.

"Oh," the pilot responded, "the wheels aren't on fire; the brakes are."

"Isn't that dangerous?"

"No," he said. "We've just recharged the battery, and we're going against the wind. We'll taxi around, and the fire will go out."

The pilot was calm, but I didn't feel very peaceful. Neither did the woman beside me. She said, "I think you should suggest that we stay in Billings tonight."

Trying to remain tactful, I said to the pilot, "Roger, do you think that it's safe for us to leave Billings tonight?"

"Don't you think that I know how to fly this plane?" he asked. "If I didn't think this was safe, I wouldn't be doing it."

I told the woman next to me, "Virginia, you ask the next time." Then, I said, "Let's pray that, if God doesn't want us to leave Billings tonight, He'll cause the plane to be unable to take off." We prayed.

I don't know how far we were from Billings when the pilot lifted the plane's wheels, but when he did, every light and electrical instrument in that plane went out. My only thought was, *The electricity took up the wheels, and we have no electricity to put them back down.* I'd never been in a plane that landed without wheels, and I really did not want to be in one. I was frightened.

The pilot asked, "Does anybody have a flashlight?"

I thought, *Who carries a flashlight around?* That's not something that I normally carry during my travels. Nobody had one. The pilot could not see the dials, and with the radio dead, he could not call in. It was raining, so there was no depth or speed perception at all. Then I heard the pilot say, "We'd better prepare for a crash landing."

At that moment, a thought struck me: *The Word will keep me.* The Lord brought to mind this precious Scripture:

> *"No weapon formed against you shall prosper, and every tongue which rises against you in judgment You shall condemn. This is the heritage of the servants of the* LORD, *and*

their righteousness is from Me," says the LORD.

(Isaiah 54:17)

You will find that when you meditate on the Word of God, He will bring Scriptures to your mind at key moments in your life. Some Scriptures that I memorize will not return to me until ten weeks later, but I've discovered that the Lord will bring them back when I really need them. He gave me that Scripture on the plane when I surely needed it.

"Behold, You desire truth in the inward parts, and in the hidden part You will make me to know wisdom" (Psalm 51:6). Truth is the Word of God. I had put truth into my spirit, and God activated it in my life, making it wisdom. If there had been nothing there to "activate," there wouldn't have been any wisdom; but that night in the plane, God's Word became wisdom and vibrant life to me.

I repeated the Scripture aloud. I said it again. What happened? The plane turned around and we landed in Billings without a problem. I saw the Word of God work with power that night.

Do you want the Word of God to work tangibly in your life? Do you want it to make you prosperous in every area of your life? Meditation is your key. Unless you commit yourself to God's answers, you cannot expect His results. You'll find His answer to whatever you need by meditating upon His Word.

4

THE "WHERE" OF MEDITATION

One of the best things about the Bible is that it provides us with practical examples, and these examples are evidence that God's Word works. I want you to see the importance of meditation and where it has been used. As we've seen, Joshua 1:8 proclaims that the key to all prosperity and success is not to let the Word depart out of your mouth, but to meditate on it, day and night, doing what it says. In fact, the history of the children of Israel is enveloped in meditation.

We tend to associate certain people with Scripture, saying, "It is their ministry to study the Word." God didn't say studying the Word was a priority only for those in the ministry. He desires His Word to be the center of *everyone's* life. Jesus emphasized this in His Word when He said, *"If you abide in My word, you are My disciples indeed. And you shall know the truth, and the truth shall make you free"* (John 8:31–32).

What does it mean to *"abide"* in the Word of God? It is meditation—memorizing, personalizing, and visualizing the Word of God. You never have to worry about whether the sun will rise in the morning or whether the moon will shine at night. Do you realize God's Word placed the sun and the moon where they are? It also keeps them there. Hebrews 1:3 says that God is *"upholding all things by the word of His power."* Continuing in the Word is very important; meditating on the Word of God is extremely important. If it is powerful enough to uphold the sun and the moon, as it did for Joshua, then it is powerful enough to take care of you.

When I first read the book of Ezra, my immediate thought was: *This is a marvelous book. Why has it taken me so long to get into something this commanding and mighty?* It demonstrates the power of the Word in the lives of individuals and nations, and it has the ability to change the entire world.

The story opens in a part of Israel's history that is critical. Before we can thoroughly understand it, however, we need to look at the events that preceded it. Joshua and his men took the Promised Land in only six-and-a-half years. Joshua was a man who meditated on the Word and didn't let it depart from his mouth. He was obedient.

The book of Judges follows Joshua and describes the early government of Israel. Then, the Bible gives the history of kings—both good and bad—and the prophets' ministry to the kings.

As we read, we see that Israel consisted of two separate kingdoms: the northern and the southern kingdoms. During this period, the Israelites began to lean increasingly on the repulsive idols of the heathen people in the land. God repeatedly warned the people of Israel about this danger, before He finally decided that enough was enough. He led King Nebuchadnezzar and the Assyrian nation in battle against the northern kingdom of Israel, and they were taken captive.

Several years later, the southern kingdom was attacked by the Babylonians, and they, too, were taken into captivity. All of Israel had been taken captive, even though, years before, the prophet Jeremiah had warned them what would happen if they did not repent.

God had used Jeremiah to tell the Jews about the horrendous penalties of idolatry. He used a group of people called the Rechabites as a visual aid in His message of warning. The Rechabites were descendants of a man named Jonadab, who had lived two hundred years prior. God gave Jonadab specific orders:

1. Don't bow down to idols.

2. Don't plant vineyards.

3. Be nomadic and do not buy land.

4. Don't drink of the vine.

Jonadab taught these rule to his children, his children's children, and so on. The Rechabites never owned land. For two hundred years, they wandered the northern kingdom with their sheep and goats and never drank wine or planted vineyards.

When Assyria attacked Israel's northern kingdom, the Rechabites weren't there. Since the area had dried up, they had taken their flocks and wandered into the southern kingdom. By doing so, they avoided the Assyrian captivity. The prophet Jeremiah warned the southern kingdom that they would taken captive by the Babylonians if they did not obey God's commands.

Jeremiah set pots on a table and filled them with wine. Then he invited all of the Rechabite leaders living in Judah to join him. "Have a drink," he told them. The Rechabites replied, "Jeremiah, you know we don't drink. God spoke to Jonadab two hundred years ago and told us not to drink. Since that day, we have never tasted of the vine." (See Jeremiah 35:5–6.)

God was using Jeremiah's demonstration to mercifully warn the people of Judah. He was saying, in effect, "Do you see that the Rechabites have obeyed My Word for two hundred years? They have never tasted of the vine, never planted vineyards, and never bought land. Now, because they have obeyed the Word, it is going to profit them."

Did you know that the Word of God is always profitable? This is right in line with the message of Joshua 1:8—the Word brings good success.

The Rechabites weren't taken captive when King Nebuchadnezzar led the Babylonians into the southern kingdom. When Nebuchadnezzar invaded, he said, "Anybody who owns land goes into captivity. Anybody who doesn't own land can stay here." And the Rechabites stayed. What can we learn from the prophet Jeremiah's message? "It pays to do what the Word says."

The Israelites were captured, and so were the people of Judah. Many of them were slaves, but don't get the idea that all of them were groveling in the ground. There were those who held esteemed positions. Ezra held a high court position, as did Nehemiah. During this same time, Esther was a queen. Notice that these Israelites were devoted servants of the Lord. When you are obedient to God, He can take care of you no matter where you are. Later, when the time came to return to Israel, many of the Jews in Babylon were so wealthy, they chose not to return. We see this in the New Testament, when the apostle Peter preached to the church at Babylon, to the Jews who had never returned to Israel.

Meditation in Captivity

Before the Israelites were taken into captivity, Jeremiah prophesied that they would be captive for seventy years.

"And this whole land shall be a desolation and an astonish-
ment, and these nations shall serve the king of Babylon seventy
years. Then it will come to pass, when seventy years are com-
pleted, that I will punish the king of Babylon and that nation,
the land of the Chaldeans, for their iniquity," says the LORD;
"and I will make it a perpetual desolation."
(Jeremiah 25:11–12)

What were the Jews in Babylon thinking during all that time? For the most part, they had their minds fastened on the Word of God. They remembered the words of the prophet: In seventy years, we get to go back. Jeremiah's prophecy was a hope, a strength, and a comfort to all those who were in captivity. We, too, have a hope, a strength, and a comfort; we can fasten our hearts on what the glorious Word has said about Jesus' return. That is a sustaining hope; and we are to comfort one another with the hope of Jesus' return. We don't know the day or the hour, but Jesus is coming back. The New Testament says that this hope is purifying. (See 1 John 3:3.)

When your thoughts are fastened to the Word of God, you are involved in a form of meditation, and the truth will both keep and sustain you.

In captivity, the children of Israel kept and obeyed God's Word to remain pure in their intent toward God. I'm sure that when the seventieth year arrived, many said, "What's going to happen? God said seventy years, and His Word cannot fail."

God had already started to prepare for the seventieth year, when His people would return to their Promised Land. I became excited when I saw how He had begun to prepare for this event one hundred fifty years earlier, through the prophet Isaiah:

Who says of Cyrus, "He is My shepherd, and he shall perform all My pleasure, saying to Jerusalem, 'You shall be built,' and to the temple, 'Your foundation shall be laid.'" Thus says the LORD *to His anointed, to Cyrus, whose right hand I have held; to subdue nations before him and loose the armor of kings, to open before him the double doors, so that the gates will not be shut: "I will go before you and make the crooked places straight; I will break in pieces the gates of bronze and cut the bars of iron. I will give you the treasures of darkness and hidden riches of secret places, that you may know that I, the* LORD, *who call you by your name, am the God of Israel."* (Isaiah 44:28–45:3)

In this prophecy, Isaiah prophesied about a man named Cyrus, a man chosen by God to set the Israelites free after their seventy-year captivity in Babylon. Before the kingdom of Babylon had ever been built, Isaiah prophesied in this passage that Cyrus would subdue that nation, which he did! Then Isaiah even described what Babylon would look like in a vision. Herodotus, supposedly the most credible historian of the Babylonian captivity, wrote that the city had two-leaved gates with bars of iron, as mentioned in the prophecy.

Why would God name Cyrus, long before his birth, and tell him that he would subdue the Babylonian kingdom? Why tell him that He would allow the temple to be rebuilt in Jerusalem? The answer is in this Scripture:

...that you may know that I, the LORD, *who call you by your name, am the God of Israel. For Jacob My servant's sake, and Israel My elect, I have even called you by your name; I have named you, though you have not known Me.*

(Isaiah 45:3–4)

God was saying, in effect, "Cyrus, I called you by name one hundred fifty years ago so that you would know that I ordained you to be the man who frees My people. You are going to free them after seventy years, according to what Jeremiah prophesied. Then you will let them rebuild Jerusalem and the temple."

Cyrus was a Persian, not a Jew. Why would he want the Jewish temple to be rebuilt? Josephus, a Jewish historian, claimed that somebody brought the book of Isaiah to Cyrus and said, "Your name is in this book."

Cyrus must have said, "Is it really? Let me see." Then, the person showed Cyrus the Scriptures and said, "The seventy years are over; you're supposed to let us return to Jerusalem and build the temple." According to Josephus, Cyrus was impressed, and he allowed the Israelites to be freed.

Josephus stated,

> For he stirred up the mind of Cyrus, and made him write this throughout all Asia: "Thus saith Cyrus the king: Since God Almighty hath appointed me to be king of the habitable earth, I believe that he is that God which the nation of the Israelites worship; for indeed he foretold my name by the prophets, and that I should build him a house at Jerusalem, in the country of Judea."[2]

The Bible concurs.

> *Now in the first year of Cyrus king of Persia, that the word of the LORD by the mouth of Jeremiah might be fulfilled, the LORD stirred up the spirit of Cyrus king of Persia, so that he made a proclamation throughout all his kingdom, and also put it in writing, saying, thus says Cyrus king of Persia: All*

---

2. Flavius Josephus, *The Works of Josephus, Complete and Unabridged* (Nashville, TN: Thomas Nelson Publishers, 1998), 286.

the kingdoms of the earth the LORD *God of heaven has given*
me. And He has commanded me to build Him a house at
Jerusalem which is in Judah.   (Ezra 1:1–2)

What stirred Cyrus' heart? What motivated him to release
the captive Israelites to return to Jerusalem? The Word of God
moved Cyrus.

Who is among you of all His people? May his God be with
him, and let him go up to Jerusalem which is in Judah, and
build the house of the LORD *God of Israel.*   (verse 3)

Cyrus not only said, "Go back to Jerusalem and rebuild the
temple"; he also said, "Any remaining Jews will pay money to help
those who are going."

King Cyrus also brought out the articles of the house of the
LORD, *which Nebuchadnezzar had taken from Jerusalem*
and put in the temple of his gods; and Cyrus king of Persia
brought them out by the hand of Mithredath the treasurer,
and counted them out to Sheshbazzar the prince of Judah.
                                          (Ezra 1:7–8)

King Cyrus gave the Jews all sorts of wealth to take back to
Judah with them. I think God must have been saying, in effect,
"Ha, ha, ha. Persia is going to pay the expenses of rebuilding the
temple in Jerusalem." It was just like the Egyptians paying for
the tabernacle when the Israelites brought their gold from Egypt
during their exodus.

Then, Ezra chapter 2 describes how all of the people prepared
to go back to Judah. They divided the people by tribes, by priest-
hoods, and by cities, and if someone didn't know quite where they
belonged, they went in a special lot, too. When they were ready to
go, there were about 300,000 of them.

This was a tremendous trip. For one thing, they had to travel way up north in order to follow the Euphrates River down through Syria and into Jerusalem. It was a journey of around one thousand miles; it took them four months to complete. Nebuchadnezzar had taken captive 600,000 Jews, and this did not include the people taken captive by the Assyrians in the northern kingdom. Certainly, people died during those seventy years; but babies were born. Still, many Jews chose not to leave Babylon, unwilling to start from scratch all over again.

When the Jews arrived in Judah, they encountered many enemies, people who had settled into the area. They were the Ammonites, Edomites, Moabites, Egyptians, and mongrel Jews, who had intermarried with some of the Assyrians (this is how the Samaritan race began to emerge).

When the Jews arrived and found people living in their land, they were unhappy and felt threatened.

Though fear had come upon them because of the people of those countries, they set the altar on its bases; and they offered burnt offerings on it to the LORD, both the morning and evening burnt offerings. (Ezra 3:3)

Notice the Jews' spiritual behavior after spending seventy years with their thoughts on the Word of God. The first thing they said was, "We need to build an altar, and God will protect us." I love that. When I read it, I thought, *They are seeking first the kingdom of God.*

These people fastened their minds to the word that came through the prophets Isaiah and Jeremiah. As they travelled that arduous long distance, what had they been doing? Obeying and fulfilling the Word of God, which had stirred their hearts.

God stirred the heart of Cyrus, and He stirred the hearts of the Israelites—with His Word. Whenever the Word supports anything, you know the foundation is secure. The Israelites built an altar, demonstrating their trust in the Lord. They started building the foundation for the temple. After it was built, there were mixed reactions. The old men cried, "Oh, this isn't the way that it used to be. It won't be as gorgeous as Solomon's temple was." (See Ezra 3:12.) They remembered how things had been in the past. However, the young men shouted for joy. "We're fulfilling the Word of God," they cried out. (See Ezra 3:13.)

When I read this, I was reminded of something I've seen in church. I've heard older people say similar things: "These days just aren't like the days when we tarried all night for the baptism of the Holy Spirit." "These people must not have what we received." That really bugs me, because the Bible says we don't receive anything through works, but only through faith. It is acting on the Word that brings anything from God. The older men were really saying, "This just isn't like the good old days." And the young men probably said, "Shut up. That's not faith; stop looking back."

It must have been an exciting adventure to be involved in the rebuilding of the temple. But then the enemy stepped in. After the temple's foundation was laid, the idolatrous people said, *"Let us build with you, for we seek your God as you do"* (Ezra 4:2). These were the mongrel Jews, along with the Ammonites, the Edomites, the Moabites, and the Egyptians, none of whom were supposed to take any part in the work of God. These people were not just saying that they wanted to help; they also wanted to bring in all of their idols, and that scared the Jews. No Jew wanted these idolaters to help. They thought, *We were sent to Babylon for seventy years because of idolatry. We don't want to go back.*

The Babylonian captivity did one thing in particular for the Jewish people. It cured them of idolatry forever, for they never involved themselves in it again. They told the people, *"You may do nothing with us to build a house for our God; but we alone will build to the LORD God of Israel, as King Cyrus the king of Persia has commanded us"* (Ezra 4:3).

The others were enraged, and the Bible says that they sat and wrote to the Persian king. The Persians tended to change kings like they changed clothes—there were three different rulers in the book of Ezra alone, and the time span wasn't long.

> *In the days of Artaxerxes also, Bishlam, Mithredath, Tabel, and the rest of their companions wrote to Artaxerxes king of Persia; and the letter was written in Aramaic script, and translated into the Aramaic language.* (Ezra 4:7)

They were saying, "Dear King Artaxerxes, do you know what the Jews are doing down here? They are rebuilding their temple. The next thing you know, they'll rebuild the walls. After that, it'll be a fortress; and before you know it, they'll rebel against you. Have you looked at the Jews' history? They're a rebellious people!"

The letter never mentioned King Cyrus' decree for the temple's rebuilding, and Artaxerxes didn't look for it. Instead, he wrote back, saying,

> *Now give the command to make these men cease, that this city may not be built until the command is given by me. Take heed now that you do not fail to do this. Why should damage increase to the hurt of the kings? Now when the copy of King Artaxerxes' letter was read before Rehum, Shimshai the scribe, and their companions, they went up in haste to*

> *Jerusalem against the Jews, and by force of arms made them*
> *cease.*   (Ezra 4:21–23)

In other words, Artaxerxes said, "Stop those Jews right now. Don't let them build one more thing. Nothing."

When the Israelites received the letter, they were discouraged and said, "Well, what's the use?" And they stopped building the temple. They were not standing on the Word at the time, and when that happens, people tend to look only at the circumstances, and they get in to trouble. They could have responded by saying, "Dear Artaxerxes, look up Cyrus's decree. We have permission to rebuild the temple." Instead, they fell apart.

That is bad news. Here's the good news: Although you may delay God's plan, you'll never do away with it. God's Word *will be* fulfilled.

For fifteen years, the Israelites stayed in Judah and had a pity party. Pity, by the way, is faith's worst enemy. They said, in effect, "We came all this distance with our children, and we can't build the temple."

Was God's Word going to get the temple built? As I read this, I thought, *If God called Cyrus by his name one hundred fifty years before he was born, His Word would complete the rebuilding of the temple. These people didn't stop God's plan; they only delayed it. And that wouldn't have happened if they had been meditating on His Word.*

During that time, God raised up two men to complete the task of rebuilding of the temple. Their names were Haggai and Zechariah. The books of Haggai and Zechariah become easier to understand when you realize they were prophesying to the people about finishing the mission. Reading the prophetic books can confuse people because they don't know the timeline of events. That is why it is easier to understand the Bible by reading it chrono-logically rather than in the order they've been placed in the Old Testament.

The prophet Haggai was an older man who had seen Solomon's temple. He said, "You know God's Word told you to complete this temple." Haggai prophesied positive words and greatly stirred the peoples' hearts. Because Haggai was a contemporary of the older people, they could not say, "Well, these kids just want to do their own thing." They had to receive his prophecies. But look at God's provision: Had He raised up only an older prophet, the young people would have written him off as an old man, dreaming dreams. But they couldn't say that because God raised up another prophet, a younger man named Zechariah, who not only had prophecies, but who also had visions.

When Haggai and Zechariah prophesied together, the Word of God touched those people and stirred their hearts. They thought, *Why aren't we building the temple, as God commanded?*

What happens when the Word of God stirs you? It triggers faith, and faith brings action. When you have faith in the Word, there will be movement, because faith produces works.

By the time the prophesying through Haggai and Zechariah took place, Persia had another king, and the Israelites wrote him a letter saying, "We have permission to rebuild the temple." They explained,

> *In the first year of Cyrus king of Babylon, King Cyrus issued a decree to build this house of God. Also, the gold and silver articles of the house of God, which Nebuchadnezzar had taken from the temple that was in Jerusalem and carried into the temple of Babylon; those King Cyrus took from the temple*

of Babylon, and they were given to one named Sheshbazzar,
whom he had made governor.   (Ezra 5:13–14)

The letter said, "Dear King Darius, we're here in Israel, and King Cyrus told us to build this temple. He even gave us money for it. We laid the foundation. Even the mongrel Jews, Egyptians, Ammonites, Moabites, and Edomites wanted to help build and bring in their idols, but we're not supposed to let them help. So, they told us to stop building and wrote a letter to King Artaxerxes, making us look bad. He told us not to build, but we already had a decree from King Cyrus. Look it up, because we're going to obey King Cyrus."

Darius looked up the decree.

Then King Darius issued a decree, and a search was made in
the archives, where the treasures were stored in Babylon. And
at Achmetha, in the palace that is in the province of Media,
a scroll was found, and in it a record was written thus: in the
first year of King Cyrus, King Cyrus issued a decree concern-
ing the house of God at Jerusalem: "Let the house be rebuilt,
the place where they offered sacrifices; and let the foundations
of it be firmly laid."   (Ezra 6:1–3)

What happened when Darius finally found these instruc-tions from King Cyrus? His heart was stirred. He wrote back and said,

Let the work of this house of God alone; let the governor of the
Jews and the elders of the Jews build this house of God on its
site. Moreover I issue a decree as to what you shall do for the
elders of these Jews, for the building of this house of God: let
the cost be paid at the king's expense from taxes on the region
beyond the river; this is to be given immediately to these men,
so that they are not hindered. And whatever they need; young

bulls, rams, and lambs for the burnt offerings of the God of heaven, wheat, salt, wine, and oil, according to the request of the priests who are in Jerusalem; let it be given them day by day without fail, that they may offer sacrifices of sweet aroma to the God of heaven, and pray for the life of the king and his sons. (Ezra 6:7–10)

He was asking all the non-Jews to start giving the Jews food and animals for their burnt offerings, that they might offer sacrifices unto God. Then, he even asked the Israelites to pray for him and his children.

Also I issue a decree that whoever alters this edict, let a timber be pulled from his house and erected, and let him be hanged on it; and let his house be made a refuse heap because of this. (Ezra 6:11)

Darius directed his attention to the enemies of the Jews, saying, "The rest of you down there, you'd better stop giving them trouble. We'll hang you if you don't stop."

When you put faith in God and His Word, circumstances will change. Haggai and Zechariah caused the Israelites to have active faith in the Word, so their circumstances had to line up accordingly. God will even move people around, if necessary. In fact, I am often shocked at how God moves people around. For instance, look at how He dealt with the heart of a young man named Ezra:

For Ezra had prepared his heart to seek the Law of the LORD, and to do it, and to teach statutes and ordinances in Israel. This is a copy of the letter that King Artaxerxes gave Ezra the priest, the scribe, expert in the words of the commandments of the LORD, and of His statutes to Israel. (Ezra 7:10–11)

Ezra was a priest, living in Babylon, who had never been in the temple; he had never made a sacrifice, and yet his first love was the law of the Lord. He must have thought, *If the Word isn't there, the people will return to idolatry.* Ezra prepared his heart to seek God through meditation, teaching, and obeying the Word of God. Then the Lord gave Ezra a burden for the hearts of the people who would worship there. He knew that the people had to be given the Word of God, or they would not endure against their enemies.

I examined historical accounts, because it often helps to make biblical stories more clear. I don't consider history to be divine; it isn't the Word of God, but it can provide helpful insights into the Bible. Historians say that when Nebuchadnezzar seized Judah, he took copies of the law, the Psalms, the Proverbs, and other poetical books, and burned them. He didn't want God's Word to enter Babylon.

But you can't destroy the Word of God, can you? One hundred years ago, someone said, "In twenty years, there won't be a Bible." You can't listen to such ridiculous talk. God knows how to protect His Word. There will always be people predicting kooky things like that, but the Bible is a worldwide best seller.

Though Nebuchadnezzar attempted to destroy God's Word, someone smuggled a copy of the Hebrew Scriptures into Babylon—it must have been a large portion of the Old Testament. It would not have contained the books of Ezra, Nehemiah, Haggai, Zechariah, or Malachi, of course, but it probably contained three-fourths of our current Old Testament. Historic accounts tell us what the wonderful priest Ezra did. He *memorized* all of it.

Ezra had a tremendous devotion to the Word of God. His name means "help." (Anybody who is as full of the Word of God as Ezra was will always be a help in any situation.) Ezra was the first scribe of the Bible. Scribes were the people who copied down God's Word. It is said that Ezra memorized the Scriptures, wrote them all down, and divided it into the Pentateuch, the historical and poetical books, the prophetical books, and so on. Ezra was the first one to categorize the Word of God; he was stirred and motivated by the Word, and he wanted the rest of the Israelites to be stirred and motivated by it, too.

He talked to the king and requested permission to return to Judah to bring God's Word to the Israelites. The king granted his consent; but that's not all he gave Ezra—he also gave him great wealth and gold to refurbish the temple. Ezra accepted these bountiful gifts, and he told the king, "There is no use in my returning to Jerusalem alone. The Word of God is in my heart, but I want to pour it into the hearts of the priests, so that they will pour it into the people's hearts."

Ezra made a call for the Jews to go back to Judah with him, and around five thousand made the journey. But among them were no priests. This disturbed Ezra. He wanted successors who would take hold of the Word. He told the people to rouse the priests, and, finally, about forty-five priests answered the call. Then Ezra said, "We will also need protection," and he called the people to fast and pray.

Isaiah 58, one of the most well-known fasting chapters in the Bible, says that fasting brings a reward, *"The glory of the* LORD *shall be your rear guard"* (Isaiah 58:8). Notice that it says that the glory of the Lord will be your *rear* guard; it protects the back of you. Ephesians chapter 6 tells Christians how to put on the armor of the Lord, a protection for the front of the body. But fasting brings protection from sneak attacks by covering the back. I believe strongly in regular weekly fasting;

and I think Christians can take a lesson from Ezra's steadfast faithfulness.

Prayer Meditation

Meanwhile, Haggai and Zechariah were prophesying, and the people began to turn to the Word of God. While they were building the temple, they sang Psalm 136:1–3 as they worked:

> *Oh, give thanks to the LORD, for He is good! For His mercy endures forever. Oh, give thanks to the God of gods! For His mercy endures forever. Oh, give thanks to the Lord of lords! For His mercy endures forever.*   (Psalm 136:1–3)

The rest of Psalm 136 rehearses what God had done for the Israelites. They were singing that song as a way of saying, "God, You helped us then, and You are helping us now." All the time they were building, the song went on, reminding them that God performed His Word in the past, and He was performing it in the present.

Again, here is prayer that says:

> *To Him who laid out the earth above the waters, for His mercy endures forever; to Him who made great lights, for His mercy endures forever; the sun to rule by day, for His mercy endures forever; the moon and stars to rule by night, for His mercy endures forever. To Him who struck Egypt in their firstborn, for His mercy endures forever; and brought out Israel from among them, for His mercy endures forever; with a strong hand, and with an outstretched arm, for His mercy endures forever; to Him who divided the Red Sea in two, for His mercy endures forever.*   (Psalm 136:6–13)

That is an effective prayer. It's scriptural to pray the way the Israelites did. This type of prayer is another form of meditation.

Meditating on What You Hear

When Ezra arrived in Judah with the Jews who traveled with him, he delivered treasures to the house of God. Then he gathered the people and started reading the Word to them. He made everybody stand while he read, and he continued for three hours. Do you think your preacher is long-winded? You wouldn't if you listened to Ezra. The listeners had not heard the Word of God for a many years. All the men, women, and children stood for hours, listening intently, as Ezra poured it into their hearts.

I have always been interested in the way priests and kings were instructed to handle the Word of God; God wants His people to have the same reverence for His Word.

First, priests were responsible to write down all of the Scriptures, as Ezra had done. Then, they were to carry the Word behind their breastplate, and when someone had a problem, they would pull out the Word and tell them what it said.

When kings were placed in office, they went to the priest and said, "Give me your copy of the Bible." (See Deuteronomy 17, 23, 31.) Then they would personally transcribe the Bible, making their own copy. The king was to read it every day, so he could judge the people appropriately. God always wanted to be the center of men's lives. He wanted His Word in a prevalent position, so the people would not get in to trouble.

Every seven years, the priest was supposed to stand before the people, as Ezra had done, and read all of the words that had been written. What was the seventh year? It was very special:

> *So Moses wrote this law and delivered it to the priests, the sons of Levi, who bore the ark of the covenant of the* LORD, *and to all the elders of Israel. And Moses commanded them, saying: "At the end of every seven years, at the appointed time in the year of release, at the Feast of Tabernacles, when all Israel comes to appear before the* LORD *your God in the place which He chooses, you shall read this law before all Israel in their hearing."* (Deuteronomy 31:9–11)

Notice they read these Scriptures during the year of release. What did Jesus say? *"If you abide in My word, you are My disciples indeed. And you shall know the truth, and the truth shall make you free"* (John 8:31–32). That is exactly what Ezra was doing; he was releasing the people from bondage by reading them God's Word.

As he read, the mongrel Jews were convicted. They said, "We've been doing some wrong things. We haven't been living right; we've lived with these idolatrous women, and we want to separate ourselves from them."

The Word of God does so many things, doesn't it? What was happening here? It was the washing of the water of the Word. (See Ephesians 5;26.) The Word began cleansing the people from sin, and a real revival started.

The Word of God brought the captives home and rebuilt their temple; the Word of God was their protection, their refreshing and cleansing. What happened? It released them.

Every time I see Ezra's name, I think, *God bless you, Ezra.* He loved the Word of God so much that he memorized it so it couldn't be destroyed. Then, he wrote it down and gave it to the people. It was passed on from generation to generation and was given to you and me.

Where to Meditate for You and Me

I find that you can meditate in any place you set your heart to do so.

One time, I was on a very early flight to Casper, Wyoming. I was meditating on Proverbs 11:30, *"The fruit of the righteous is a tree of life, and he who wins souls is wise."* As I was spiritually chewing on these words, the Lord spoke to my spirit. saying, *Wouldn't you like to win a soul to Christ?*

I looked around the plane. At that early hour, almost every seat was vacant. I thought, *Who, Lord?*

His response to me was, *How about the flight attendant?*

As she served coffee, God opened her heart to the *Four Spiritual Laws* tract,[3] which I had studied earlier.

You may find that the same Scriptures you meditate on one day will be used in fantastic ways that same day. I've discovered that if you really desire something, you will whatever is required to attain it. If you want to be successful in every area of life, then you'd better meditate on the Word of God. Perhaps you can't start out memorizing five verses a day; but you can learn one verse every other day, can't you?

When God told Joshua to meditate on the Word, He was saying, "I want you to be saturated, completely soaked, with the Word of God: keep it in your mind, your mouth, and your actions." Joshua became an example of God's living Word in action—and so can you. Joshua was over eighty, and a very busy man, as we've seen. As I studied him, I thought, *I wonder what he meditated on. Did he pick Proverbs?*

---

3. Bill Bright, *The Four Spiritual Laws* (Peachtree City, GA: Campus Crusade for Christ, 2007).

The first year I began meditating God's Word, I memorized Proverbs. It was so exciting that I thought everybody should memorize them. I even made my children start memorizing the book. My son really complained, saying, "There isn't a mother in our church that's making her kids memorize the book of Proverbs." Then, he really started crying the blues. He said, "There isn't a mother in this city that makes her children memorize Proverbs. I doubt there's a mother in the nation!" I decided to stop him before he got to the world, so I said, "Oh, honey, how fortunate you are to have me for your mother. You have the only mother in the nation who makes you memorize. Aren't you pleased?"

The only books that were written when Joshua meditated on Scripture were the first five books of the Bible, or the Pentateuch (or Torah), which was written by Moses and consisted of Genesis, Exodus, Leviticus, Numbers, and Deuteronomy. How would you like to memorize Leviticus? Yet that is what Joshua meditated on, day and night.

Once when I was teaching on meditation, a man came up to me after the service and said, "Marilyn, I am eighty-three years old. I started meditating on God's Word when I was twenty-six." He started quoting chapter after chapter of the gospel of Matthew. I listened to him quoting the Word, and I cannot tell you what happened to me spiritually. It seemed as though my spirit jumped up and said, "Whee!" The Bible says that hearing the Word brings faith. (See Romans 10:17.) My hearing of the meditated Word of God coming out of that man's mouth was "faith hearing."

I asked him, "Are you retired?"

"Retired? Do I look retired? I am a professor at a university, and I'll never retire. I'll teach until I die."

I thought, *Of course. All of the Word inside of him is filling him, jam-packed with God's life.* That man was also prosperous in every single area. I thought, *Oh God, I wish I'd started meditating at the age of twenty-six.* It's like exercise; it's never too late to begin.

The bathtub is a good place to say your Scriptures aloud. Sometimes, I ride a bike and rehearse them. David meditated on his bed. (See Psalm 63:6.) Everyone has a perfect place.

5

THE "HOW" OF MEDITATION

I want to share what I wrote about my method of meditation in my recent book *Your Pathway to Miracles*:

> The following is the method I used. I took Proverbs 6:22 as my guide, which talks about taking the teachings of one's parents to heart: "When you walk, they will guide you; when you sleep, they will watch over you; when you awake, they will speak to you" (NIV).
>
> I decided to begin in the morning, corresponding to the phrase, "When you awake, they will speak to you." So, when I got up each day, I would say my memory verse ten times.
>
> In the afternoon, I would say the verse one time, in conjunction with the phrase, "When you walk, they will guide you."

Then, at night, I would recite my verse once before going to bed, and I would say the verse for the next day one time, in relation to the phrase, "When you sleep, they will watch over you." It's been said that the last thing you hear at night goes through your mind seven times.[4]

The Absolute First

As I said earlier, as you get out of bed, your mind is at its freshest and cleanest. It's like a blackboard without writing. Why waste it on anything other than God's Word? Even before I brush my teeth, I meditate on the Word. Because your mind is uncluttered with cares and thoughts, you'll find that you begin to grasp the Scriptures as never before.

Then, sometime during the day, review the Scriptures again and ponder them. Say them aloud, several times. Refresh your mind as to what you're memorizing.

Later, before you go to sleep, say them in bed. Say them several times. Let's review that passage from Proverbs that we read in chapter 2. These are precious verses that explain how the Scriptures will rule your spirit when you meditate on them:

> *My son, keep your father's command, and do not forsake the law of your mother. Bind them continually upon your heart; tie them around your neck. When you roam, they will lead you; when you sleep, they will keep you; and when you awake, they will speak with you.*　　　　(Proverbs 6:20–22)

---

4. Marilyn Hickey, *Your Pathway to Miracles* (New Kensington, PA: Whitaker House, 2011), 76.

The Word of God will keep you. I believe that when God's Word is continually fresh in your spirit through meditation, it will protect you throughout the day and during the night.

Select the Material

The first step in getting started with meditation is to select the book of the Bible you want to study. Notice I said *book*, not *verse* or *chapter*. There are plenty of short books, if you don't want to tackle one of the longer ones. You might begin with Jude or Colossians.

For this book, I have included verses arranged by topic that can prepare you to memorize entire books of the Bible. I started memorizing by learning a verse each day. Even that small amount of Scripture quickened my mind, and I began increasing the amount I memorized. Eventually, I was up to fifteen verses each day. The Word of God will quicken you, so don't get discouraged. Start small, and you can be assured that your meditation will grow easier, if you stick with it. Think of it as a physical exercise. You begin with a few push-ups or a short jog, and then you gradually increase your workout each day until, before you know it, you are buff and running long distances.

After you've selected the material, choose the number of verses you want to learn for that day. Start with an amount that is comfortable for you, even if it's only a verse each day. Be sure to set a daily goal for yourself and consistently meet those goals.

Choose a Partner

I think having a partner is wonderful. Lately, my busy travel schedule has made it hard for me to meditate with same partner, but I've had some great partners over the years. I would recommend that you choose one. You don't need to have long conversations each day, just go over your verses together. When you know that you have to call your partner in the morning with memorized Scripture, you'll be more diligent about it. Even when your mind is tired and fuzzy, you'll get those Scriptures in.

I won't kid you. There are times when you'll feel discouraged. Some days, the devil says to me, *Why are you going through all this effort? What are you trying to accomplish?* But if you have a partner, you will have someone to encourage you when your meditation becomes a struggle.

When I meditated on the book of Proverbs, I breezed through a few chapters. Then I got to a chapter that was a struggle to get through. I found the same thing happened when I read some of the psalms. Psalms 63 and 64 were easy, but another chapter made me wonder whether I'd ever get through it. A partner will help you keep the pace when you're discouraged. If you fall behind, that's okay. Fall behind. You have the rest of your life.

A Chapter at a Time

I like to meditate on one chapter at a time before I go on to the next. I do not totally review a book. I'm not memorizing so that I can say, "I can quote thirty-one chapters of Proverbs, if you have enough time." The purpose of meditation is to get the Word into your spirit so that it can become wisdom in your life. If I'm learning four verses at a time, and the chapter has twelve verses, then I'll have memorized the whole chapter on the third day.

Refresh Past Meditations

Wherever I happen to be meditating, I like to read a verse from books that I've meditated on previously. When you finish one book and move on to another, look back occasionally and review what you've meditated on in the past.

Why meditate on the Word? Because God said it would bring success into every area of your life. God's Word is going to dominate your thought life, your emotional responses, and your attitudes. You will be, as Joshua was, a living epistle to others. When someone talks with you, the Holy Spirit will begin quickening those memorized Scriptures to your mind, and you'll think, *He needs this Scripture; it just fits him.*

Keep a Notebook

This is another practice you'll find both helpful and encouraging. Carry around a small notebook and write down the revelations the Lord gives to you. If you don't write them down, you'll likely forget them. Through meditation, you'll discover that your spirit becomes more alive than ever before, and a notebook will come in handy to record those moments of fresh revelation. Because you are making the Word of God precious in your life, you'll find the Lord revealing more to you than ever before. If you're ever in a place of discouragement regarding your memorization, read your notebook past revelations, and let them be an encouragement.

Prescription of Meditation

My soul shall be satisfied as with marrow and fatness, and my mouth shall praise You with joyful lips. When I remember

You on my bed, I meditate on You in the night watches.
(Psalm 63:5–6)

People will say to me, "I'm starving for the Word in my church. I get no spiritual food, and my pastor isn't much of a preacher." Psalm 63 says you are supposed to remember the Lord and meditate on *Him*; don't rely on your pastor for all of your spiritual food. This Scripture says your soul will get *fat* and your mouth will be *full of praise* when you meditate on the Lord.

Notice, too, that the psalmist's meditation was at night. Have you ever noticed that problems seem to loom ten times larger at night? I'm not one to wake up in the middle of the night, but when I do, it's usually because of a difficult circumstance. It's then that my problems look like mountains. That's the time to meditate on the Word of God.

At a seminar in Schenectady, New York, I remember thinking that every possible thing that could go wrong seemed to be hitting me all at once: finances, family, radio ministry, and so on. I also had a terrible pain and a swollen area, from which red streaks were starting to appear. I prayed, and said, "I am not going to be moved by those symptoms." I went through my memory verses, but I still could not sleep because of the pain.

When I travel, I carry audio versions of the New Testament with me, and I finally said, "All right, devil, you're going to be sorry for keeping me awake." After about an hour of listening to the Word, the soothing quality of it caused me to fall back asleep. I turned the cassette off and said, "Father, it's not my problem. I cast my cares on You."

In the morning, there weren't any red streaks, and two days later, the swelling was gone, too. The Word works.

As I noted in the beginning, Psalm 119:11 says, *"Your word I have hidden in my heart, that I might not sin against You!"* Fair enough.

The action, *hiding the word*, and the reason, *so as not to sin against God*, are captured in this one short verse. How do we do this?

Again, here are a few simple tips:

1. Gather a collection of Scripture passages you desire to meditate upon. I would suggest the books Ephesians or Colossians. (I began with Proverbs and loved every minute spent there.) Or, as I stated, you can start with a few verses. I have included some examples for you later in the book.

2. Decide on a certain portion to memorize each day—one verse a day, one verse every other day, or two verses. Begin at a comfortable pace.

3. Select a partner, someone who desires to meditate on the same material. Call your partner daily and rehearse the Scripture. Keep your telephone conversation short.

I want to stop here and take a moment to share an experience about one of my previous prayer partners. When I started to meditate, I decided I needed to find a partner. I thought that in case I ever felt the urge to stop meditating, or I became discouraged, a partner would keep me encouraged. It seemed like a good way to start; so I prayed, "Lord, who would You have me to be partners with?" The Lord spoke to me, and it was not the person I wanted Him to choose. It was a person who attended our church, who tended to gripe a lot. Whenever she came in the room, you felt like you wanted to be somewhere else, because if she got hold of you, it took half an hour for her to tell you all of her problems. Then she'd look you up later, because she hadn't finished telling you about them.

The Lord said to me, *I want her to be your meditation partner.*

I thought, *Oh Lord, anybody but her.* I thought she would spend the time griping, and we wouldn't be able to get through the verses. Then I thought, *Oh, she'll probably say no.* So, I called and said, "For the rest of my life, I'm going to meditate on the Word of God. I'll start in Proverbs, and I would like you to be my partner for that book, if you will."

"Yes," she said. "I want to be your partner."

I arranged to call her at seven each morning and told her I wouldn't be able to talk for very long because my children had to go to school.

The next morning, when I called, she immediately started griping.

"Let's go over our verses," I said.

"No," she answered. "I need to tell you this first. I am so depressed."

"I don't have time, because my children have to get to school," I replied, and we proceeded to go over our Bible verses.

Over the next two weeks, every time I called this lady, she wanted to gripe, but I didn't have time for griping, so we would go over Scriptures we wanted to meditate on, and that's all. By the third week, however, something had happened. I called her the first morning of the third week, and instead of griping, this lady said, "I got the most marvelous thing out of this chapter. Did you get this?" Then she shared the revelation she received from the Word, and it was so exciting. From that day forward, her whole attitude had changed.

Some time afterward, my husband asked, "What happened to that woman? She used to be the most negative person I've ever seen."

I said, "I can tell you what happened to her. The Word of God started coming out of her mouth through meditation—and it changed her." And it can change you, too.

Okay, let's continue with tips on meditation:

1. Encourage one another—especially if you get behind.

2. Keep a notebook on the revelations you receive while meditating.

3. Be sure to memorize the chapter and verse of the book you're memorizing when studying verses alone. It's good to know the where the Scripture is found.

4. Don't get discouraged.

Meditation is the way we hide the Word of God in our hearts and receive the benefits mentioned in Psalm 119:11, Joshua 1:8, and numerous other passages in the Bible.

You can hide the Word, and when you seek it, you'll find something rich and more rewarding than a child's game. You'll find the key to a blessed, prosperous, and successful life.

I'll be honest—when I began studying Joshua 1:8, I was troubled. I thought, *Lord, You are telling me here and in Psalm 1 to meditate on Your Word day and night—but have You seen my schedule? I'm busy. I'm a mother, a pastor's wife; and then there is the radio and television ministry, along with writing and traveling. How can I possibly meditate on Your Word day and night? You must not understand my schedule.* Then the Lord began dealing with me about Joshua's schedule. He said, *Did you know that Joshua was responsible for the food, water, clothing, and spiritual and military guidance for over a million people?* Think about that. While the Israelites had been in the wilderness, God provided everything: food (manna), clothing that didn't wear out, heat and air-conditioning (the pillar of cloud and fire), military protection, and water. God met every provision of the children of Israel while they were wandering in the wilderness. After they crossed the Jordan River, this provision was made Joshua's responsibility.

Joshua had a tremendous sense of accountability and a very busy schedule. The Lord said to me, *You get nervous if ten people come over for dinner. What if you had a million people to feed every day? That's a conservative figure.* I thought, *Well, Lord, if You are telling me to meditate, I'd better find out more.*

6

HEALING FOR A NEW GENERATION

A few years ago, one of my friends was delighted to give birth to a beautiful baby girl. She and her husband were elated to have their own child, because they'd been unable to have children for the past fifteen years of their marriage, despite numerous doctor visits and referrals to various experts. After their baby girl was born, the pediatrician noticed an abnormality with her spine and scheduled some extensive testing. It was discovered that their baby had a spinal condition that required some dangerous and costly surgeries. My friend and her husband were heartbroken. Their thoughts and emotions ran the gamut, a mixture of faith, anger, doubt, frustration, hope, confusion, and more. Thankfully, these parents are people of faith, and they decided that, no matter how they felt or what they thought, and regardless of the doctor's evaluations, they were going to pray and believe that Jesus would heal their baby girl. They received lots of prayer and support from pastors, friends, and family members near and far.

Before the surgery, the doctors did a final MRI to gain any more information regarding the baby's spinal condition that would help the surgeon. The parents had been told that the MRI wouldn't take long, perhaps fifteen minutes in total. As the MRI was under way, the parents still were praying and trusting God to heal their baby girl.

After thirty minutes, a technician came to tell them that another MRI was needed to verify the findings of the first one. He asked the parents to wait patiently for it to be completed. Finally, after ninety minutes, and multiple MRIs and inquiries, the doctor himself came to report that they were unable to find the spinal abnormality that had been found in the previous diagnosis. While the doctor and technician were perplexed, the parents were ecstatic and thrilled beyond description! Not only had Jesus given them the miracle of a baby girl, but He also had healed her of a horrible spinal condition!

I love hearing these kinds of testimonies. I love getting to see Jesus do such amazing miracles and healings. It's always breath-taking, and I never want to take for granted the healing power of God in our modern lives.

Here's another fun testimony from when I first started in the ministry. When I was in my early twenties—before I had kids—my mom did a series of meetings with my husband and me in Wales. We were having a fantastic time ministering to and connecting with the wonderful Welsh people. During a daytime teaching session, I felt that God wanted me to pray for people who had ear or hearing problems. Being new in the ministry, and quite an amateur with all the healing stuff, I was hesitant to obey what I felt to be God's leading. Nevertheless, I felt God nudging me, so I decided to go out on a limb. Besides, I probably wouldn't see these people ever again.

I asked anyone with hearing or ear problems to stand. After sharing a brief testimony of a healing that I had heard about, I prayed for them while they stood at their seats. There wasn't any healing line, there wasn't any music playing in the background, and I didn't get myself "worked up." It was just a simple and straight-forward prayer, during which I was thinking, *God, you had better do Your stuff! It's Your name and reputation on the line!* I'd been clear in my presentation that Jesus is the healer and not me, which is the absolute truth. After praying, I asked those standing to check their ears, and many of them were pleasantly surprised to find that they had been healed! But there was one lady who seemed agitated. After a minute or so, she began to wave her hand enthusiastically, so I asked her what had happened. She quickly blurted out that Jesus had healed her ear. I nodded and was happy for her. But then she grew more emphatic about her healing and went on to explain that she had been born deaf in one ear. She seemed to be in her late thirties or early forties, and this was the first time in her life that she could hear out of that ear. She exhibited over-the-top excitement!

Initially, I didn't believe her, because I was just an amateur at healing, and I thought that the "big" miracles were a product of only the more professional grade of ministry, not for us "newbies." Nevertheless, in my disbelief, I checked the woman's ears myself; indeed, she was healed. I was in such disbelief that I asked her if there had been anyone with her who could verify that she had truly been deaf in that ear prior to the prayer. It was almost as if I was trying to talk her out of her healing. A friend who had accompanied her to the morning session verified that she had always spoken to the woman in her good ear, because she had been stone-deaf in the other ear. Needless to say, I was flabbergasted, and to this day, I'm always amazed at God's healing power!

I never want to take for granted God's healing power, and I never want to trivialize His presence, power, miracles, and demonstrations. I always want to experience amazement and awe at what

God does and who He is, and to be grateful for His work—never becoming dull or indifferent.

The principle of gratitude is extremely important when it comes to healing. Remember Jesus' response to one of the ten lepers whom He had cleansed from leprosy. They had lived on the outskirts of town because their leprosy made them a threat to the healthy population. As such, they were treated as social outcasts, not to mention how they must have looked and smelled! When they saw Jesus and understood who He was, they began shouting at Him, asking Him to cleanse them from their disease—which is exactly what He did! He healed them all and told them to go and show themselves to the priests who had banished them from the temple. But it is interesting that only one of the ten lepers, a foreign Samaritan, returned to Jesus to express his gratitude. Based on Jesus' reaction, it's clear to see that He was disappointed in the other nine. In reply, Jesus told this lone standout, *"Arise, go your way. Your faith has made you well"* (Luke 17:19). Perhaps this former leper was cleansed on the inside as well as the outside, from the horror and rejection of this horrific disease.

Be Thankful

This brings me to an important point on the topic of healing: the significance of being thankful. This is an extremely valuable principle that pertains to virtually every area of our lives. Thankfulness should not be confined to a Thursday in November or when something magnificent happens in your life. It's a good habit to practice being thankful for all things, big and small.

I've seen the principle of gratitude applied in a healing context, and I've observed some interesting results. I've seen situations in which a person has received a small degree of healing, but not enough for his or her entire need. Generally speaking, people who remain thankful for small things tend to receive more complete and more frequent healings than those who complain about how other people received a more complete healing than they did. Let's strive to pass the gratitude test, regardless of what we see or how we feel.

Have Faith

Another important point that has particular relevance for our healing topic is faith—an essential ingredient for healing. One of the miracles in Jesus' life that always takes my breath away is the story of the lady who had an issue of blood for twelve years.

According to Scripture, she had spent all of her money on doctors but only continued to get worse. She was in a desperate condition. She was so desperate that she risked going out in public when it was against Jewish law for a woman suffering her type of malady to do so. She could have been stoned for violating this law. But the Bible tells us that she told herself, *If I can touch the hem of Jesus' garment, I'll be healed.* And that is exactly what happened. (See Luke 8:43–48.)

As Jesus passed through the crowd, on His way to heal someone else, this woman pressed forward to touch the hem of His garment. Jesus felt power leave Him, and He stopped and asked who had touched Him. This woman sheepishly stepped out and admitted her action, to which Jesus replied (similar to how He responded to the Samaritan leper), *"Your faith has made you well. Go in peace"* (Luke 8:48).

In my own life, I find that faith is more of a choice than a feeling. If I go with my feelings, I succumb to unbelief and doubt without much effort or time. But choosing faith is the noble and commendable decision. Anyone can doubt; exceptional people choose to believe. So let's decide together that we will be believers rather than doubters.

Come to Jesus, the Complete Healer

These stories have shown us that being thankful and having faith are important keys to receiving healing. But as we look at Jesus' ministry on earth, we can make some additional observations that can be applied to our lives today.

When we look at Jesus' works, we see that He didn't heal people only physically, but He also healed them in other ways—emotionally, relationally, and so on. One of the reasons this is significant is because I don't think there's a person on the planet who doesn't need healing in some fashion or form. Some need physical healing, while others need emotional healing. Some need relational healing, while others need healing from their past. Fortunately, Jesus is the complete Healer.

When I read in the Gospels about Jesus' work, it seems to me that He was always healing, whether it was restoring sight, raising dead children back to life, cleansing lepers, healing fevers, or casting out demons. Jesus restored wholeness to virtually everyone with whom He interacted, except for perhaps the religious leaders of His day who resented His ministry, but that's for a different book. So, when we think about healing, let's remember that Jesus is our complete Healer.

One of the most powerful healings in Jesus' ministry involved the Samaritan woman at the well, which we read about in John chapter 4. This woman came to the well at an unusual time of the day to draw water, a time when the fewest number of people would be around. Jesus was sitting by the well at this time, tired from His journey. When she arrived, Jesus asked her for a drink of water. This was only the beginning of an absolutely revolutionary conversation between these two individuals. You see, in Jesus' day, Jewish men were forbidden to talk with women, especially foreign, idol-worshipping Samaritan women. By merely speaking with this woman, Jesus broke several of the social norms of His day.

As you read through this conversation between Jesus and the Samaritan woman, you'll see that He was almost baiting her to enter into a deeper discussion, until He finally told her to summon her husband. She curtly replied, *"I have no husband"* (John 4:17). Jesus proceeded to reveal to her that she had five husbands, and that the man with whom she was currently living wasn't her husband. In this observation, Jesus exposed the woman's painful secret—the very reason she had come to draw water when the fewest people were present. Her reply revealed her shame. There was no escaping that Jesus knew her dark and painful secret.

At the end of their conversation, Jesus revealed a "secret" of His own.

The woman said to Him, "I know that Messiah is coming" (who is called Christ). "When He comes, He will tell us all things." Jesus said to her, "I who speak to you am He."
(John 4:25–26)

This visit with the Samaritan woman occurred quite early in Jesus' ministry. I find it completely amazing that He would reveal such an intimate fact about Himself to a Samaritan woman who was living in sin! It always takes my breath away!

After her conversation with Jesus, the woman returned to her village and told the men, *"Come, see a Man who told me all things that I ever did. Could this be the Christ?"* (John 4:29). You must know that there were many men who wanted to see the man whom this Samaritan woman was taking about! And so many villagers believed, and they went to see who this guy was.

*So when the Samaritans had come to Him, they urged Him
to stay with them; and He stayed there two days. And many
more believed because of His own word.*   (John 4:40–41)

After Jesus' stay in the village, many more people became followers, all because He'd had a conversation with a woman who
suffered from extremely broken relationships.

When we invite Jesus into our brokenness—into our pain,
hurt, and sickness—our chances of getting healed dramatically
improve, simply because Jesus is the Healer. When I look at Jesus'
life in the Gospels, it seems to me that He healed almost everywhere He went.

From this story about the Samaritan woman at the well, we
see that Jesus healed through conversation. Perhaps it's time for us
to have open, honest, and transparent dialogue with Jesus, so that
He can do some amazing healings in the broken areas of our lives.

Jesus also healed by laying His hands on people—on blind
eyes, deaf ears, lepers, and even dead people. Jesus also healed
through what I would call "declaration." An example of this would
be when He sent Jairus' servant back to the home, telling him—or
declaring—that Jairus' daughter was well. (See Luke 8:50.)

Jesus healed people in some rather funky ways, as well. With
one blind man, He spit in the dirt, made mud, and put it on his
eyes; then Jesus told him to go and wash it off. When the man
returned, he could see again. (See John 9:1–7.) In another instance,
Jesus spit directly on a blind man's eyes. (See Mark 8:22–26.)
That's pretty unusual. Of course, we can't get too wrapped up in a
certain method or system of healing simply based on the diversity
of ways in which Jesus healed during His ministry. Perhaps He
healed in so many different ways so that we would know that our
focus must remain on the Healer and not on a particular system
or method.

As you go through this book, be sure that you do not shut yourself off to Jesus healing you in different areas and in different ways. Let's be sure that we remain open to Jesus healing our physical bodies, while also giving Him the freedom to heal our relationships, our emotions, our paradigms, our sense of self-worth, and even the scars of past memories. He is able to heal all of our brokenness, pain, diseases, hang-ups, and dysfunctions. Sometimes, the healing we so desperately need in our bodies starts when Jesus heals our emotions, relationships, and dysfunctions.

No matter what our need, Jesus is our complete Healer.

7

MEDITATIONS ON HEALING

1. Healing Is the Bread of the Children

In Matthew chapter 15, a mother comes to Jesus in need of healing for her demon-possessed daughter. This Canaanite woman refuses to take offense at the disciples' coldness or at the words of Jesus when He says to her, *"It is not good to take the children's bread and throw it to the little dogs"* (Matthew 15:26). Instead, she presses in for her healing, saying, *"Yes, Lord, yet even the little dogs eat the crumbs which fall from their masters' table"* (verse 27). Jesus responds by complimenting her faith: *"O woman, great is your faith! Let it be to you as you desire"* (verse 28). This undaunted woman, who was considered a "dog" by the Jews, said that even little puppies can eat the crumbs that fall from the table. She was willing to pick up a few "crumbs off the floor" for her daughter. Although this woman wasn't a Jew, Jesus honored her persistent faith, and the child was healed.

We can give up too soon by looking at our symptoms and pain rather than at God's Word.

Scripture Memorization #1

"And in that day you will ask Me nothing. Most assuredly, I say to you, whatever you ask the Father in My name He will give you. Until now you have asked nothing in My name. Ask, and you will receive, that your joy may be full."
—John 16:23–24

2. Healing Is Provided in the Atonement

Isaiah 53 lists several ways in which God provides healing for us.

1. He took our rejection.

2. *"He is despised and rejected by men"* (Isaiah 53:3).

3. He took our anxiety.

4. *"Surely He has borne our griefs and carried our sorrows"* (verse 4).

5. He took our transgressions and iniquities.

"He was wounded for our transgressions, He was bruised for our iniquities; the chastisement for our peace was upon Him, and by His stripes we are healed" (verse 5).

When you were born again, you acknowledged that Jesus took your place and was punished for all your sin, but did you understand that He carried it all *away*? In showing you what Jesus did with sin, I want to show you what Jesus did with sickness. Jesus carried away your transgressions and your iniquities so that you would no longer have to bear them. Are you supposed to go back into your past and pick up the burden and guilt of your various sins? Does the Holy Spirit come to remind you of your sins—"You smoked," "You took drugs," "You lied," or whatever? Of course not! The Holy Spirit comes to set you free and to let you know that your sin has been carried away, *"as far as the east is from the west"* (Psalm 103:12).

Jesus is our double cure in that He took on both our sins *and* our sicknesses. By His wounds, we have been healed.

Scripture Memorization #2

"...who Himself bore our sins in His own body on the tree, that we, having died to sins, might live for righteousness; by whose stripes you were healed."
—1 Peter 2:24

3. Our Healing Will Quickly Appear

One of the names of God is *Jehovah Rapha,* which means "the Lord our Healer," or "the Lord our Health." Healing is a part of God's nature. He gave this revelation of His name to Moses, who lived in health for one hundred twenty years. (See Deuteronomy 34:7.)

Moses refused to go anywhere without God's presence. In fact, God promised Moses that he would never be without the presence of God Almighty: *"My Presence will go with you, and I will give you rest"* (Exodus 33:14).

Likewise, God promises us that our healing will come quickly.

Scripture Memorization #3

"Then your light shall break forth like the morning, your healing shall spring forth speedily, and your righteousness shall go before you; the glory of the LORD shall be your rear guard."
—Isaiah 58:8

4. Multiple Blessings Will Be Ours

There is a woman in Scripture who could not be cured by doctors. Even when she was mentioned in the Bible, she was not named. In a sense, she was a nobody, a person to be seen and forgotten.

However, this woman was not a nobody in *faith*.

Suddenly, a woman who had a flow of blood for twelve years came from behind and touched the hem of His garment. For she said to herself, "If only I may touch His garment, I shall be made well."   (Matthew 9:20–21)

This woman's faith came by hearing. (See Romans 10:17.) Then she spoke her faith and acted on her faith. And in the end, she received her total healing.

Jesus turned around, and when He saw her He said, "Be of good cheer, daughter; your faith has made you well." And the woman was made well from that hour.   (verse 22)

Jesus not only healed the woman, but He also multiplied her blessing by giving her a name. He called her *"daughter."*

Scripture Memorization #4

"Surely blessing I will bless you, and multiplying I will multiply you."
—Hebrews 6:14

5. Specific Healing

Blind Bartimaeus received a miracle in his eyes. As he sat begging on the roadside, he heard that Jesus was passing by, and he called out to Him, *"Jesus, Son of David, have mercy on me!"* (Mark 10:47). Jesus asked him, *"What do you want Me to do for you?"* (verse 51). He wanted Bartimaeus to identify his specific need.

Be specific when you pray, and you will get specific results! Broad, general prayers, which I call "generic" prayers, may shake things a little, but they don't bring results. If you pray for nothing in particular, that's exactly what you'll get—nothing in particular! The more specific you are when you ask for healing in faith, the more specific the results will be. It is very important to identify the problem or situation you are praying for by faith. Be specific in the way that you pray, and be specific about what you pray for. Both are very important.

When you go before God in prayer, you must believe for some particular thing. Jesus expected this of others in the biblical record, as well—Blind Bartimaeus is just one example. Bartimaeus threw off the coat that represented his blindness. (See Mark 10:50.) He put total trust in Jesus and received his healing.

Scripture Memorization #5

"Bless the LORD*...who forgives all your iniquities, who heals all your diseases."*
—Psalm 103:2–3

6. Humility for Healing

When Isaiah, one of God's prophets, told King Hezekiah that he would die, the leader cried out to God in a desperate prayer.

"Remember now, O LORD, I pray, how I have walked before You in truth and with a loyal heart, and have done what was good in Your sight." And Hezekiah wept bitterly.

(2 Kings 20:3)

As Isaiah was leaving, the Lord gave him a new message of healing for Hezekiah.

Return and tell Hezekiah the leader of My people, "Thus says the LORD, the God of David your father: 'I have heard your prayer, I have seen your tears; surely I will heal you.'"

(verse 5)

What changed God's mind? The king humbled himself, and God honors the humble. (See, for example, James 4:6.)

Scripture Memorization #6

*"For assuredly, I say to you, whoever says to this mountain,
'Be removed and be cast into the sea,' and does not doubt in
his heart, but believes that those things he says will be done,
he will have whatever he says."*
—Mark 11:23

7. "Crazy Faith" Friends

We need faith-filled friends. In Capernaum, Jesus saw the faith of four friends of a paralytic man. When the men realized that they could not get their disabled friend near Jesus because of the large crowd, they were forced to improvise, and their act of faith was amazing.

> *When they could not come near Him because of the crowd, they uncovered the roof where He was. So when they had broken through, they let down the bed on which the paralytic was lying.* (Mark 2:4)

Imagine dragging a paralyzed man onto a roof and then cutting a hole in the roof to lower him by rope into the building. Uncommon faith produces uncommon results.

> *When Jesus saw their faith, He said to the paralytic, "Son, your sins are forgiven you."* (verse 5)

The forgiveness of sins and the healing of our bodies go together. This is the double miracle.

Are you a "crazy faith" friend? Crazy faith attracts other "crazy faith" friends.

Scripture Memorization #7

"God anointed Jesus of Nazareth with the Holy Spirit and with power, who went about doing good and healing all who were oppressed by the devil, for God was with Him."
—Acts 10:38

8. Healing and Casting Out Demons

Some sicknesses are caused directly by demon possession. In one case, an epileptic man came to Jesus, who rebuked and cast out a demon from the man. (See Matthew 17:15–18.)

Then He healed many who were sick with various diseases, and cast out many demons.   *(Mark 1:34)*

You cannot be a spiritual vacuum; either you will fill your soul with the spiritual things of God, or Satan will fill you with things from his spirit realm. Never forget that if the devil can find a place in you, he will take it!

The devil and his demons tremble at the name of Jesus. (See James 2:19.) So, don't be afraid to cast out demons in the name of Jesus. It isn't our name that provides the power but His. I have seen His name deliver people all around the world. And Jesus gave the same authority to us.

Scripture Memorization #8

"And these signs will follow those who believe: in My name they will cast out demons; they will speak with new tongues; they will take up serpents; and if they drink anything deadly, it will by no means hurt them; they will lay hands on the sick, and they will recover."
—Mark 16:17–18

9. God's Will Regarding Healing

The first healing recorded in Matthew is that of a man healed of leprosy. He said to Jesus, *"Lord, if You are willing, You can make me clean"* (Matthew 8:2). Jesus responded, *"I am willing; be cleansed"* (verse 3). Likewise, He is willing to heal you of all diseases. Jesus came to earth to do the Father's will. (See, for example, Hebrews 10:7.) And when He ascended to heaven, He left no physical possessions behind, only the authority of His name.

If we are going to be healed, we must first be convinced that it is God's will to heal. I know a family whose members were committed Christians, but they were sick all the time. The children were so consistently ill that the mother joked about having a regular appointment at the doctor's every week. Then this woman was invited to one of my first Bible studies and heard the Word of God regarding healing. Soon, she was convinced that healing was part of the salvation package that Jesus purchased for us at Calvary. This lady started praying the Word over her children and rebuking the enemy, and she saw sickness flee every time. Years later, she could say that, except for regular checkups, none of her children had seen a doctor in years. She and her family learned not only how to be healed but also how to walk in divine health.

It was God's will to heal people when Jesus was on earth. And it is still His will to heal. We are beneficiaries of Christ's estate, for *"Christ [is] in [us], the hope of glory"* (Colossians 1:27). God wants all to be saved and healed.

Scripture Memorization #9

"He sent His word and healed them, and delivered them from their destructions."
—Psalm 107:20

10. A Miracle in Our Hands

Jesus spoiled every funeral He attended, including His own.

The laying on of hands can be the transferring of a miracle. Jesus laid His hands on Jairus' dead daughter, and she was raised from the dead. (See Mark 5:21–24, 35–43.)

In another instance, Jesus laid hands on all who were brought to Him one day as the sun was setting. All of them experienced healing from their various diseases—not *some* of them but *all* of them! (See Luke 4:40.)

Although Jesus' power was limited in His hometown of Nazareth, His hometown, He was still able to lay hands on the sick and heal them. (See Mark 6:5.) And after Paul was shipwrecked on the island of Malta, he laid hands on a man suffering from a fever, and the man was healed. (See Acts 28:8.)

If you have Jesus in your heart, you also have miracles of healing within your hands.

Scripture Memorization #10

"For they are life to those who find them, and health to all their flesh."
—Proverbs 4:22

11. Faith, the Currency of Heaven

I have found that God responds to faith, not need. Faith is the currency of the kingdom of heaven.

[Jesus said,] *"And many lepers were in Israel in the time of Elisha the prophet, and none of them was cleansed except Naaman the Syrian."* (Luke 4:27)

Here, Jesus was referencing the story of Naaman, a commander of the Syrian army who was also a leper. He traveled to Israel in search of healing, and the prophet Elisha sent his servant to Naaman, instructing him to wash in the Jordan River seven times in order to be physically restored. At first, Naaman refused, insisting that the rivers in Syria were superior. But finally, one of his servants said to him, *"My father, if the prophet had told you to do something great, would you not have done it? How much more then, when he says to you, 'Wash, and be clean'?"* (2 Kings 5:13). So Naaman went to the Jordan and dipped himself into the waters seven times, *"and his flesh was restored like the flesh of a little child, and he was clean"* (verse 14). He received his miracle.

Keep praying. Keep believing. Miracles provide a witness to unbelievers. People need to see powerful demonstrations of God's Word and His love. Miracles performed in Jesus' name will spark faith within the hearts of unbelievers.

Scripture Memorization #11

"And whatever things you ask in prayer,
believing, you will receive."
—Matthew 21:22

12. Anointing with Oil for Healing

Anointing with oil is another way in which God heals the sick. It works by "the law of transference."

> *Is anyone among you sick? Let him call for the elders of the church, and let them pray over him, anointing him with oil in the name of the Lord.*   (James 5:14)

David wrote of God's anointing oil:

> *You anoint my head with oil; my cup runs over.*
>   (Psalm 23:5)

David was well aware of this practice, because it was common for shepherds to apply oil to the wounds of their beloved sheep. It helped to heal wounds and also to drive away flies.

Oil represents the healing presence of the Holy Spirit. We need God's anointing to give life to our bodies. We need education for our minds, but we need anointing for them, as well.

Make sure that you attend a church that supports the anointing of the sick with oil, and have faith that God will bring healing to all those who need it.

Scripture Memorization #12

"It shall come to pass in that day that his burden will be taken away from your shoulder, and his yoke from your neck, and the yoke will be destroyed because of the anointing oil."
—Isaiah 10:27

13. Healing as a Process

Sometimes healing is more of a process than an event.

Mark 8:22–26 tells of a blind man from Bethsaida who came to Jesus for healing. But receiving his healing was a process. Instead of providing instant healing, Jesus first spit in the man's eyes and then put His hands on him. When asked if he could see anything, the man said, *"I see men like trees, walking"* (Mark 8:24). Then Jesus placed His hands on the man's eyes and made him look upward. After this, the man could see clearly. (See verse 25.)

I believe that Jesus was actually spitting on the man's blindness. Jesus hated, and still hates, what blindness does to people.

Remember—sometimes, healing takes time.

Scripture Memorization #13

"Being confident of this very thing, that He who has begun a good work in you will complete it until the day of Jesus Christ."
—Philippians 1:6

14. Healer or Destroyer?

Uhat about Job's sickness?

You may remember the book of Job, in which a poor man is smitten with disease, famine, financial collapse, and other hardships. The truth is, God did not make Job sick; the devil did. (See Job 2:7.)

When Job was stricken with disaster, everyone blamed God. Job's wife blamed God (see verse 9), and Job's friends blamed God (see, for example, Job 8:3–4; 11:6). But despite his afflictions, Job continued to put his trust in God, saying, *"For I know that my Redeemer lives, and He shall stand at last on the earth"* (Job 19:25).

At the end of the book, God responds to Job's prayers. He not only heals Job, but He also restores his wealth and doubles his life span. (See Job 42.)

It turns out that God is not a destroyer; He is a healer.

Scripture Memorization #14

"The thief does not come except to steal, and to kill, and to destroy. I have come that they may have life, and that they may have it more abundantly."
—John 10:10

15. Confessing Healing

Confession is speaking aloud the things you believe in your heart. Jesus overcame Satan by quoting the Word (see Matthew 4:4, 7, 10; Luke 4:4, 8, 12), and this is the way we can overcome the enemy, too. Possession comes by confession.

I continually confess that, according to Romans 8:11, the Spirit of Him who raised Jesus from the dead dwells in me, and He who raised Christ from the dead is quickening, or giving life to, my mortal body by His Spirit who dwells in me. There is nothing quite as valuable as personalizing the promises of God.

At one time, I had a tumor in my breast. I spoke to my breast, saying that God's Word was health to my flesh. I confessed this every hour for twenty-four hours. By the end of those twenty-four hours, the tumor had disappeared.

Scripture Memorization #15

"And they overcame him by the blood of the Lamb and by the word of their testimony, and they did not love their lives to the death."
—Revelation 12:11

16. Paul's Thorn

And lest I should be exalted above measure by the
abundance of the revelations, a thorn in the flesh was
given to me, a messenger of Satan to buffet me, lest I
be exalted above measure.
—2 Corinthians 12:7

Was Paul's *"thorn in the flesh"* a literal sickness? Some scholars believe that Paul had a problem with his eyesight. But Scripture tells us that Paul wrote long letters with his own hand. (See Galatians 6:11.) Paul never referred to his thorn as a physical ailment, but he clearly expressed that it was a messenger from Satan.

In Numbers 33:55, God speaks to the Israelites and calls the Canaanites *"thorns in your sides."* In Joshua 23:13, they are called *"thorns in your eyes."* In both cases, these thorns refer to personalities and not circumstances.

Perhaps a demon stirred up the persecution Paul seemed to encounter everywhere he went. Perhaps, like the Israelites, Paul's thorn was a demonic personality and not a sickness.

Scripture Memorization #16

"My people are destroyed for lack of knowledge."
—Hosea 4:6

17. Listen and Obey

In John 5, a paralytic was healed of a chronic disease. He had been paralyzed for thirty-eight years, and he was lying beside a pool that was said to heal people when the water was stirred.

> *For an angel went down at a certain time into the pool and stirred up the water; then whoever stepped in first, after the stirring of the water, was made well of whatever disease he had.*   (John 5:4)

Because only the first person in the pool would be healed, the paralytic man waited patiently for someone to come along and push him into the pool at the crucial moment when the angel stirred the water. Jesus saw the man and instantly knew of his condition. He asked the man, *"Do you want to be made well?"* (John 5:6). Then, Jesus gave the man a three-part command.

"Rise…" (verse 8). This would be an act of great faith.

"…take up your bed…" (verse 8). Assuming the man were able to get on his feet, now he would have to stoop down and pick up his bed.

"…and walk" (verse 8). Now, he would have to carry both himself and his bed.

Then we read, *"And immediately the man was made well, took up his bed, and walked"* (verse 9).

Be like the paralytic man. Listen to the voice of Jesus and act in faith.

Scripture Memorization #17

"Beloved, I pray that you may prosper in all things and be in health, just as your soul prospers."
—3 John 2

18. Shake Off the Devil

In Acts 28, we read about Paul's encounter with a venomous snake. While shipwrecked on the island of Malta, Paul was bitten by a snake that was hiding in a bundle of sticks he had collected for a fire. Those who saw the reptile latch onto Paul's hand assumed that he was a murderer, *"whom, though he has escaped the sea, yet justice does not allow to live"* (Acts 28:4).

But Paul simply shook the snake off his hand and into the fire and suffered no ill effect. (See verse 6.) After witnessing this, the people of the island brought their sick to Paul for healing.

Follow Paul's example. Don't let the enemy poison you. We have authority over the devil. Shake him off and go about your day.

Scripture Memorization #18

"Behold, I give you the authority to trample on serpents and scorpions, and over all the power of the enemy, and nothing shall by any means hurt you."
—Luke 10:19

19. Authority to Heal

In Matthew 8, Jesus healed the servant of a centurion. Despite the fact that the centurion was not a Jew (he was a military commander), he recognized authority when he saw it, and he had faith in the words Jesus spoke. The centurion said,

> *Lord, I am not worthy that You should come under my roof. But only speak a word, and my servant will be healed. For I also am a man under authority, having soldiers under me. And I say to this one, "Go," and he goes; and to another, "Come," and he comes; and to my servant, "Do this," and he does it.*   (Matthew 8:8–9)

Jesus *"marveled"* (verse 10) at the man's faith and then healed his servant.

Can you heed the authority of God's Word over the voice of your symptoms?

At age twenty-six, I was told that I would never have a child, because my ovaries were too small. However, my husband and I believed that God had authority over the situation and could do the impossible. Ten years later, I went to a doctor because I was having symptoms of pregnancy. After examining me, the doctor said I was going through changes but that I was definitely *not* pregnant.

Five months later, I gave birth to my daughter, Sarah. God— not doctors or other medical "experts"—is the final authority on everything, including our health.

Scripture Memorization #19

"For God has not given us a spirit of fear, but of power and of love and of a sound mind."
—2 Timothy 1:7

20. Group Miracles

Can God perform group miracles? In the New Testament, Jesus multiplied loaves and fish for over five thousand men, not counting the women and children. (See Matthew 14:15–21; Mark 6:31–44; Luke 9:10–17; John 6:5–15.)

Let's take a look at another example of a group miracle.

Then [the Israelites] *journeyed from Mount Hor by the Way of the Red Sea, to go around the land of Edom; and the soul of the people became very discouraged on the way. And the people spoke against God and against Moses: "Why have you brought us up out of Egypt to die in the wilderness? For there is no food and no water, and our soul loathes this worthless bread." So the* LORD *sent fiery serpents among the people, and they bit the people; and many of the people of Israel died. Therefore the people came to Moses, and said, "We have sinned, for we have spoken against the* LORD *and against you; pray to the* LORD *that He take away the serpents from us." So Moses prayed for the people. Then the* LORD *said to Moses, "Make a fiery serpent, and set it on a pole; and it shall be that everyone who is bitten, when he looks at it, shall live." So Moses made a bronze serpent, and put it on a pole; and so it was, if a serpent had bitten anyone, when he looked at the bronze serpent, he lived.*   (Numbers 21:4–9)

Of course, the bronze serpent was representative of Jesus being lifted up on a cross, taking away the sins and sicknesses of the world. So when the church looks upon the Lord in faith, she will be healed. The faith of a mustard seed can move mountains. (See Matthew 17:20.) So, yes, even little faith can produce great miracles—for individuals as well as for large groups.

Scripture Memorization #20

"Assuredly, I say to you, if you have faith as a mustard seed, you will say to this mountain, 'Move from here to there,' and it will move; and nothing will be impossible for you."
—Matthew 17:20

21. An Everlasting Covenant of Healing

After the Israelites were delivered from slavery in Egypt, God made a covenant with them. Covenants represent a legally binding agreement that lasts a lifetime, as long as the terms of the covenant are kept. Some biblical examples of covenants are found in Exodus 15:26 and 23:25 and in Deuteronomy 7:15.

God kept His covenant with the Israelites, as shown in Psalm 105:

> *For He remembered His holy promise, and Abraham His servant. He brought out His people with joy, His chosen ones with gladness. He gave them the lands of the Gentiles.*
> (Psalm 105:42–44)

Jesus redeemed us from the curse of the law. (See Galatians 3:13.) We have a covenant—a lifetime agreement—of healing and health, through Jesus Christ.

Scripture Memorization #21

> *"Christ has redeemed us from the curse of the law, having become a curse for us (for it is written, 'Cursed is everyone who hangs on a tree').*"
> —Galatians 3:13

22. Faith, No Matter What

Why is it that we pray for some people, and they still die?

This is a big question. Some of us stumble over it and stop praying for the sick.

I went through some dark times over this issue. Then, God gave me the example of the three Hebrew men in the furnace, found in Daniel 3. They refused to bow down and worship Nebuchadnezzar, the Babylonian king. Despite the threat of dying in a furnace, they believed that God would deliver them. That is great faith.

However, they also told the king that if God didn't deliver them, *"we do not serve your gods, nor will we worship the gold image which you have set up"* (Daniel 3:18).

Through that verse, God spoke to me, saying, "I am pouring faith and faithfulness within you. Will you still pray for the sick, even when it seems that your faith has failed?"

Scripture Memorization #22

"For this reason we also, since the day we heard it, do not cease to pray for you, and to ask that you may be filled with the knowledge of His will in all wisdom and spiritual understanding."
—Colossians 1:9

23. An Open Door for Sickness

Repentance is the great key to living in health. Bitterness and unforgiveness leave an open door for sickness and disease to remain, even in the lives of believers. Soul "sickness" is often the result of choosing to hold on to anger or bitterness without forgiving others or oneself. Guilt is a terrible tormentor.

Many years ago, I became very angry over a situation. A certain person had pulled some bad business deals on people in our church congregation. Although the matter had been handled, I began to meditate on it; the more I meditated on it, the angrier I became. Shortly after that, I came down with severe flu symptoms: sore throat, fever, and the like. The Lord showed me how I had opened the door to sickness by allowing bitterness to lodge in my heart. What the person had done was wrong, but I needed to leave the matter to God. Needless to say, I repented of my sin and slammed the door on the sickness—and received my healing!

Scripture Memorization #23

"I am the light of the world. He who follows Me shall not walk in darkness, but have the light of life."
—John 8:12

24. Gifts of Healings

As you'll see in the memory verse below, one of the nine gifts of the Spirit is healing. And notice that this gift is plural—"*gifts of healings.*"

I believe there is a gift of healing for every disease. Often, when we have been healed of a certain disease, we develop the faith to pray for others who are stricken with the same disease. Some Christians have a special gift of praying for the sick.

When we pray for others to be healed, we also need to tell Satan that he cannot bring back disease a second time. Based on God's words in Nahum 1:9—"*Affliction will not rise up a second time*"—we should understand two things: (1) sickness may try to return, but (2) it is never the Lord's will for this to happen.

Scripture Memorization #24

"For to one is given the word of wisdom through the Spirit,
to another the word of knowledge through the same Spirit, to
another faith by the same Spirit, to another gifts of
healings by the same Spirit."
—1 Corinthians 12:8–9

25. The Laying On of Hands

The laying on of hands is another way to heal the sick.

Jairus wanted Jesus to lay hands on his dying daughter. He believed in the laying on of hands for healing.

> [Jairus said to Jesus,] *"My little daughter lies at the point of death. Come and lay Your hands on her, that she may be healed, and she will live."*   (Mark 5:23)

There is power in personal touch, and Jairus was convinced of this. In this case, however, Jesus was interrupted, and the girl died before He could go to her. (See Mark 5:25–35.) But Jesus was undeterred by the news of her death, and He continued on to Jairus' house. When Jesus finally arrived, *"He took the child by the hand, and said to her, 'Talitha, cumi,' which is translated, 'Little girl, I say to you, arise.' Immediately the girl arose and walked"* (Mark 5:41–42).

When a leper begged for healing, *"Jesus, moved with compassion, stretched out His hand and touched him….Immediately the leprosy left him, and he was cleansed"* (Mark 1:41–42).

Scripture is clear that Christians, as Jesus' followers and imitators, *"will lay hands on the sick, and they will recover"* (Mark 16:18).

Scripture Memorization #25

"And whatever you ask in My name, that I will do, that the Father may be glorified in the Son. If you ask anything in My name, I will do it."
—John 14:13–14

26. Standing Firm

Why do some people lose their healing? Because they do not stand firm.

Stay in constant contact with your Healer. Stand firm against the enemy. Remember, the devil is a thief. (See John 10:10.) If Satan is reminding you of your past, remind him of his future. You overcome the devil by speaking promises to him from God. Speak God's Word to lying symptoms of illness.

Just as the Lord has made provision for sins committed by believers, He has made provision for the physical ailments of believers. Over and over in the Old and New Testaments, God has given us promises for the healing of our bodies. We should all be growing in the knowledge of the Lord, and that *knowledge contained in the Word* gives us greater and greater power to live a sinless life in a healthy body. However, we must exercise that power. Change your mind about sickness! Change what you say about sickness! Don't just expect to be healed if you are ill; expect to walk in complete health. You have the nature of the One who is *never sick*, just as surely as you have the nature of the One who *never sins*.

Scripture Memorization #26

"What do you conspire against the LORD? He will make an utter end of it. Affliction will not rise up a second time."
—Nahum 1:9

27. Instant Healing

We who are indwelled by the Holy Spirit have a built-in repair shop to frequent.

In Acts, the Jews from Antioch and Iconium *"stoned Paul and dragged him out of the city, supposing him to be dead"* (Acts 14:19). Although beaten and bruised, Paul got back up and reentered the city. Then, the next day, he and Barnabas walked twenty-five miles to the city of Derbe. This is a man who had been beaten and stoned. I believe that Paul was raised from the dead. But, whether he had died or not, Paul certainly received a miraculous and instantaneous healing.

Can the Holy Spirit perform instant repairs on us as we go about our lives? I believe He can and does. If we need it, the Holy Spirit will provide instant service.

Scripture Memorization #27

"But if the Spirit of Him who raised Jesus from the dead dwells in you, He who raised Christ from the dead will also give life to your mortal bodies through His Spirit who dwells in you."
—Romans 8:11

28. Our Pressure Neutralizer

Pressure can make us sick. But joy neutralizes pressure.

In Acts 16, Paul and Silas were in prison, and they were praying and singing hymns. Meanwhile, these two men had just had their backs ripped open with a scourge, they had been placed in irons in the deepest dungeon of a Philippian jail, and it was midnight! What's more, they were innocent men. Even the most "turned-on" Christian might find such a situation a time to moan and groan—at least a little. And yet, in the midst of their difficulties, Paul and Silas sang praises to the Lord because they *knew* their God.

> *But at midnight Paul and Silas were praying and singing hymns to God, and the prisoners were listening to them. Suddenly there was a great earthquake, so that the foundations of the prison were shaken; and immediately all the doors were opened and everyone's chains were loosed.*
>
> (Acts 16:25–26)

Although beaten and chained, their joy freed them of the bondage of fear and discouragement.

Scripture Memorization #28

"Now to Him who is able to do exceedingly abundantly above all that we ask or think, according to the power that works in us, to Him be glory in the church by Christ Jesus to all generations, forever and ever. Amen."
—Ephesians 3:20–21

29. All Kinds of Healing

Gifts of healings are spiritual equipment. Once again, remember that the word *"gifts"* in Paul's passage on spiritual gifts is plural. (See 1 Corinthians 12:9.)

It appears that certain people will have greater success in some areas of healing than others. I have seen healings of all kinds. However, I see the greatest success when I pray for people with tumors. My husband called me a "growth, tumor, and wart woman." Those are my specialties. Other believers may share this gift, and still others have different gifts of healing.

God has many ways to heal. Keep your faith in Him.

Scripture Memorization #29

"Therefore we do not lose heart. Even though our outward
man is perishing, yet the inward man is being renewed
day by day."
—2 Corinthians 4:16

30. Don't Give Up on Your Healing

Sometimes, it seems healing is long in coming.

I remember that Dr. David Yonggi Cho, who pastors the largest church in the world, said that he believed in his healing from tuberculosis for nineteen years before it finally manifested.

I like fast manifestations of healing. Who doesn't? However, we cannot give up in due season. We reap if we don't faint. (See Galatians 6:9 KJV.) When you *feel* as if God is a million miles away and life is a downer, are you going to give up? No, when you are wholly committed to God, your emotions belong to Him. If you feel upbeat, that's great. But if you feel down, it doesn't make any difference; God will come through for you, so hold on to your faith. Every one of us experiences disappointments. But you don't have to give the enemy any opportunity in your life just because your emotions are on a roller coaster. Command your emotions to get in line with God's Word and remain steady!

Eventually, Dr. David Yonggi Cho was totally healed of tuberculosis, because he never gave up.

Scripture Memorization #30

"For the Scripture says, 'Whoever believes on Him will not be put to shame.'"
—Romans 10:11

ABOUT THE AUTHORS

Marilyn Hickey

As founder and president of Marilyn Hickey Ministries, Marilyn is being used by God to help cover the earth with the Word. Her Bible teaching ministry is an international outreach via television, satellite, books, CDs, DVDs, and healing meetings. Marilyn has established an international program of Bible and food distribution, and she is committed to overseas ministry, often bringing the gospel to people who have never heard it before.

Marilyn's message of encouragement to all believers emphasizes the fact that today can be the best day of your life if Jesus Christ is living in you.

Marilyn, along with her late husband, Wallace Hickey, founded the Orchard Road Christian Center in Greenwood Village, Colorado. She has two grown children, five grandchildren, and four great-grandchildren.

Sarah Bowling

Sarah Bowling, the daughter of Marilyn Hickey, is vice president of Marilyn Hickey Ministries and cohost of the internationally broadcast television program *Today with Marilyn and Sarah*. She is the founder of Saving Moses, a humanitarian initiative dedicated to reducing infant mortality throughout the world. She is also a guest speaker at seminars, conferences, and college campuses worldwide. Sarah and her husband, Reece, are senior pastors of Orchard Road Christian Center. They have three children and live in the Denver area.

Meditation #1

"And in that day you will ask Me nothing. Most assuredly, I say to you, whatever you ask the Father in My name He will give you. Until now you have asked nothing in My name. Ask, and you will receive, that your joy may be full."
—John 16:23–24

Meditation #2

"...who Himself bore our sins in His own body on the tree, that we, having died to sins, might live for righteousness; by whose stripes you were healed."
—1 Peter 2:24

Meditation #3

"Then your light shall break forth like the morning, your healing shall spring forth speedily, and your righteousness shall go before you; the glory of the LORD shall be your rear guard."
—Isaiah 58:8

Meditation #4

"Surely blessing I will bless you, and multiplying I will multiply you."
—Hebrews 6:14

Meditation #5

"Bless the LORD...who forgives all your iniquities, who heals all your diseases."
—Psalm 103:2–3

Healing Is the Bread of the Children

We can give up too soon by looking at our symptoms and pain rather than at God's Word.

Healing Is Provided in the Atonement

Jesus is our double cure in that He took on both our sins and our sicknesses. By His wounds, we have been healed.

Our Healing Will Quickly Appear

One of the names of God is *Jehovah Rapha*, which means "the Lord our Healer," or "the Lord our Health." Healing is a part of God's nature.

Multiple Blessings Will Be Ours

Jesus not only healed the woman with the issue of blood in Matthew 9, but He also multiplied her blessing by giving her a name. He called her "daughter."

Specific Healing

Be specific when you pray, and you will get specific results! Broad, general prayers, which I call "generic" prayers, may shake things a little, but they don't bring results.

Meditation #6

"For assuredly, I say to you, whoever says to this mountain, 'Be removed and be cast into the sea,' and does not doubt in his heart, but believes that those things he says will be done, he will have whatever he says."
—Mark 11:23

Meditation #7

"God anointed Jesus of Nazareth with the Holy Spirit and with power, who went about doing good and healing all who were oppressed by the devil, for God was with Him."
—Acts 10:38

Meditation #8

"And these signs will follow those who believe: in My name they will cast out demons; they will speak with new tongues; they will take up serpents; and if they drink anything deadly, it will by no means hurt them; they will lay hands on the sick, and they will recover."
—Mark 16:17–18

Meditation #9

"He sent His word and healed them, and delivered them from their destructions."
—Psalm 107:20

Meditation #10

"For they are life to those who find them, and health to all their flesh."
—Proverbs 4:22

Humility for Healing

In 2 Kings chapter 20, King Hezekiah humbled himself, and God healed him. God honors the humble.

"Crazy Faith" Friends

In Capernaum, Jesus saw the faith of four friends of a paralytic man. When the men realized that they could not get their disabled friend near Jesus because of the large crowd, they were forced to improvise, and their act of faith was amazing. "Crazy faith" attracts other "crazy faith" friends.

Healing and Casting Out Demons

The devil and his demons tremble at the name of Jesus. So, don't be afraid to cast out demons in the name of Jesus. It isn't our name that provides the power but His.

God's Will Regarding Healing

It was God's will to heal people when Jesus was on earth. And it is still His will to heal. We are beneficiaries of Christ's estate, for "*Christ* [is] *in* [us], *the hope of glory*" (Colossians 1:27). God wants all to be saved and healed.

A Miracle in Our Hands

The laying on of hands can be the transferring of a miracle. If you have Jesus in your heart, you also have miracles of healing within your hands.

Meditation #11

*"And whatever things you ask in prayer, believing,
you will receive."*
—Matthew 21:22

Meditation #12

*"It shall come to pass in that day that his burden will be
taken away from your shoulder, and his yoke from your neck,
and the yoke will be destroyed because of the anointing oil."*
—Isaiah 10:27

Meditation #13

*"Being confident of this very thing, that He who has begun a
good work in you will complete it until the day of Jesus Christ."*
—Philippians 1:6

Meditation #14

*"The thief does not come except to steal, and to kill, and to
destroy. I have come that they may have life, and that they
may have it more abundantly."*
—John 10:10

Meditation #15

*"And they overcame him by the blood of the Lamb and by the word
of their testimony, and they did not love their lives to the death."*
—Revelation 12:11

Faith, the Currency of Heaven

I have found that God responds to faith, not need. Faith is the currency of the kingdom of heaven.

Anointing with Oil for Healing

Anointing with oil is another way in which God heals the sick. Oil represents the healing presence of the Holy Spirit. We need God's anointing to give life to our bodies. We need education for our minds, but we need anointing for them, as well.

Healing as a Process

Sometimes healing is more of a process than an event.

Healer or Destroyer?

You may remember the book of Job, in which a poor man is smitten with disease, famine, financial collapse, and other hardships. The truth is, God did not make Job sick; the devil did. It turns out that God is not a destroyer; He is a healer.

Confessing Healing

Confession is speaking aloud the things you believe in your heart. Jesus overcame Satan by quoting the Word, and this is the way we can overcome the enemy, too.

Meditation #16

"My people are destroyed for lack of knowledge."
—Hosea 4:6

Meditation #17

*"Beloved, I pray that you may prosper in all things and be in
health, just as your soul prospers."*
—3 John 2

Meditation #18

*"Behold, I give you the authority to trample on serpents and
scorpions, and over all the power of the enemy, and nothing
shall by any means hurt you."*
—Luke 10:19

Meditation #19

*"For God has not given us a spirit of fear, but of power and
of love and of a sound mind."*
—2 Timothy 1:7

Meditation #20

*"Assuredly, I say to you, if you have faith as a mustard seed,
you will say to this mountain, 'Move from here to there,' and
it will move; and nothing will be impossible for you."*
—Matthew 17:20

Paul's Thorn

Paul never referred to his thorn as a physical ailment, but he clearly expressed that it was a messenger from Satan.

Listen and Obey

Be like the paralytic man in John 5:6–9. Listen to the voice of Jesus and act in faith.

Shake Off the Devil

Follow Paul's example when he shook off the snake in Acts 28. Don't let the enemy poison you. You have authority over the devil. Shake him off and go about your day.

Authority to Heal

Jesus healed the servant of a centurion. Despite the fact that the centurion was not a Jew (he was a military commander), he recognized authority when he saw it, and he had faith in the words Jesus spoke. Can you heed the authority of God's Word over the voice of your symptoms?

Group Miracles

When the church looks upon the Lord in faith, she will be healed. The faith of a mustard seed can move mountains. Even little faith can produce great miracles— for individuals as well as for large groups.

Meditation #21

"Christ has redeemed us from the curse of the law, having become a curse for us (for it is written, 'Cursed is everyone who hangs on a tree')."
—Galatians 3:13

Meditation #22

"For this reason we also, since the day we heard it, do not cease to pray for you, and to ask that you may be filled with the knowledge of His will in all wisdom and spiritual understanding."
—Colossians 1:9

Meditation #23

"I am the light of the world. He who follows Me shall not walk in darkness, but have the light of life."
—John 8:12

Meditation #24

"For to one is given the word of wisdom through the Spirit, to another the word of knowledge through the same Spirit, to another faith by the same Spirit, to another gifts of healings by the same Spirit."
—1 Corinthians 12:8–9

Meditation #25

"And whatever you ask in My name, that I will do, that the Father may be glorified in the Son. If you ask anything in My name, I will do it."
—John 14:13–14

An Everlasting Covenant of Healing

Jesus redeemed us from the curse of the law. We have a covenant—a lifetime agreement—of healing and health, through Jesus Christ.

Faith, No Matter What

God is pouring faith and faithfulness within you. Will you still pray for the sick, even when it seems that your faith has failed?

An Open Door for Sickness

Repentance is the great key to living in health. Bitterness and unforgiveness leave an open door for sickness and disease to remain, even in the lives of believers.

Gifts of Healings

One of the nine gifts of the Spirit is healing. And notice that this gift is plural—*"gifts of healings."* I believe there is a gift of healing for every disease.

The Laying On of Hands

There is power in personal touch. Scripture is clear that Christians, Jesus' followers and imitators, *"will lay hands on the sick, and they will recover"* (Mark 16:18).

Meditation #26

"What do you conspire against the LORD *He will make an utter end of it. Affliction will not rise up a second time."*
—Nahum 1:9

Meditation #27

"But if the Spirit of Him who raised Jesus from the dead dwells in you, He who raised Christ from the dead will also give life to your mortal bodies through His Spirit who dwells in you."
—Romans 8:11

Meditation #28

"Now to Him who is able to do exceedingly abundantly above all that we ask or think, according to the power that works in us, to Him be glory in the church by Christ Jesus to all generations, forever and ever. Amen."
—Ephesians 3:20–21

Meditation #29

"Therefore we do not lose heart. Even though our outward man is perishing, yet the inward man is being renewed day by day."
—2 Corinthians 4:16

Meditation #30

"For the Scripture says, 'Whoever believes on Him will not be put to shame.'"
—Romans 10:11

Standing Firm

Why do some people lose their healing? Because they do not stand firm. You overcome the devil by speaking promises to him from God. Speak God's Word to lying symptoms of illness.

Instant Healing

Can the Holy Spirit perform instant repairs on us as we go about our lives? I believe He can and does. If we need it, the Holy Spirit will provide instant service.

Our Pressure Neutralizer

Pressure can make you sick. But joy neutralizes pressure.

All Kinds of Healing

Gifts of healings are spiritual equipment. Once again, remember that the word *"gifts"* in Paul's passage on spiritual gifts is plural. (See 1 Corinthians 12:9.) God has many ways to heal. Keep your faith in Him.

Don't Give Up on Your Healing

Sometimes, it seems healing is long in coming. Every one of us experiences disappointments. But you don't have to give the enemy any opportunity in your life just because your emotions are on a roller coaster. Command your emotions to get in line with God's Word and remain steady!